Group Process Guidelines
for Leading Groups and Classes

© 2009, Center for Psychiatric Rehabilitation, Trustees of Boston University. All rights reserved.

All rights reserved. No part of this publication may be reproduced or transmitted in any form or by any means, electronic or mechanical, including photocopying, recording, or any information storage or retrieval system—except for the purchaser's individual use—without permission in writing from the publisher.

Published by:

Center for Psychiatric Rehabilitation
College of Health and Rehabilitation Sciences (Sargent College)
Boston University
940 Commonwealth Avenue West
Boston, MA 02215
http://www.bu.edu/cpr/

The Center for Psychiatric Rehabilitation is partially funded by the National Institute on Disability and Rehabilitation Research and the Center for Mental Health Services, Substance Abuse and Mental Health Services Administration.

All proceeds from the sale of this book are used to further the work of the Center for Psychiatric Rehabilitation. No royalties are paid to the authors.

ISBN: 978-1-878512-43-7

Group Process Guidelines
for Leading Groups and Classes

LeRoy Spaniol, Sue McNamara, Cheryl Gagne, and Rick Forbess

Boston University Center for Psychiatric Rehabilitation

Group Process Guidelines for Leading Groups and Classes is a resource for leaders and teachers of knowledge-based or skill-based groups and classes in mental health and self-help settings.

These guidelines also may be used to supplement other curricula and workbook products published by the Center for Psychiatric Rehabilitation, including:

Technology for Training Practitioners

Rehabilitation Readiness Training Technology
Setting an Overall Rehabilitation Goal Training Technology
Functional Assessment Training Technology
Direct Skills Teaching Training Technology
Case Management Training Technology

Workbooks for the Psychiatric Rehabilitation Process

Activities for Assessing & Developing Readiness for Rehabilitation Services
Abriendo Caminos en Tu Vida
Career Planning Curriculum

Workbooks for Recovery Groups

Recovery Workbook: Practical Coping and Empowerment Strategies
Recuperando la Esperanza—Libro Práctico
Recovery Workbook 2: Connectedness

Training Materials for Teaching Skills

Food Education for People with Serious Psychiatric Disabilities

Training Materials for Working with Families

What Professionals Need to Know about Families
The Role of the Family in Psychiatric Rehabilitation

Visit http://www.bu.edu/cpr/products/ for a complete listing and descriptions of products available from the Center for Psychiatric Rehabilitation.

Leadership remains an art as well as a science—some of the tools of leadership are not simply the tools of science—some are the tools of self.

William A. Anthony,
from *Principled Leadership in Mental Health Systems and Programs*, 2008

Contents

Preface 1

Chapter 1	**Planning for the Group Activity**	3
1.1	Identifying the Group Structure and Roles	4
1.2	Identifying the Group Participants	10
1.3	Identifying the Group Objectives	14
1.4	Organizing the Activity Materials	15
1.5	Preparing Yourself	25
1.6	Arranging the Environment	27
	Checklist: Planning for the Group Activity	29

Chapter 2	**Conducting the Group Activity**	30
2.1	Reviewing the Group Structure and Roles	31
2.2	Reviewing the Group Objectives	32
2.3	Orienting to the Activity	32
2.4	Giving Directions	35
2.5	Presenting the Activity Content	36
2.6	Presenting to Individuals within a Group	36
2.7	Modifying the Content and/or Pace	37
2.8	Summarizing the Group Activity	40
	Checklist: Conducting the Group Activity	41

Chapter 3	**Encouraging Participation**	43
3.1	Facilitating Introductions	44
3.2	Attending to the Participants	46
3.3	Engaging the Participants	47
3.4	Responding to the Participants	50
3.5	Responding to Implicit Communication	54
3.6	Acknowledging Contributions	54
3.7	Dealing with Challenging Behaviors	55
3.8	Promoting Problem-Solving	58
3.9	Promoting Self-Understanding	60
3.10	Critiquing Participation and Progress	61
	Checklist: Encouraging Participation	64

© 2009, Trustees of Boston University. All rights reserved. Center for Psychiatric Rehabilitation.

Chapter 4		**Promoting Peer Leadership**	**66**
	4.1	Encouraging Peer-to-Peer Interactions	67
	4.2	Self-Disclosing	69
	4.3	Incorporating Experiences into Content	74
	4.4	Collaborating with Peers	75
	4.5	Supporting Peer Leaders	78
		Checklist: Promoting Peer Leadership	81
Chapter 5		**Following Up the Group Activity**	**82**
	5.1	Evaluating the Group Activity	83
	5.2	Assessing Experiences with Participants	84
	5.3	Identifying Future Activities	85
	5.4	Recording Progress Notes or Other Documentation about Group Members' Participation	86
		Checklist: Following Up the Group Activity	88

Conclusion 89

References 90

Preface

A wide variety of classes and groups are used in mental health and self-help settings. Many classes and groups are knowledge-based or skill-based, involving teaching information about content areas, such as coping and stress management. Some examples of groups that are knowledge-based or skills-based include psychoeducation groups, skills teaching groups, and recovery-oriented groups, some of which are based on *The Recovery Workbook* (Spaniol, Koehler & Hutchinson, 1994, 2009) or the *Wellness Recovery Action Plan* (WRAP) (Copeland, 2000). Other groups provide enrichment activities, such as wellness skills, peer support and counseling, and discussion groups.

While some leaders are skilled in teaching or in group process, many group leaders lack sufficient training and experience in facilitating groups and classes effectively. Many group leaders are new to the process of leading groups; and many group leaders were never formally trained in the skills of conducting a group, but rather they learned how to run a group on-the-job by observing a co-worker or a supervisor. This book provides some guidelines for teachers and leaders of groups that are knowledge-based or skills-based, but they are not designed for facilitating a support or therapy group.

Regardless of the type of group being led, all groups require the leaders to perform skills *before* the group in preparation for the group or class, *during* the group while conducting the group or teaching the class, and *after* the group for following-up the group or class activities. This book is organized into sections that outline these preparation, delivery, and follow-up skills. Information is included that explains this series of group process skills as well as some examples and exercises to practice the skills. Throughout the book you will be asked to think of a group or class that you currently lead or are planning to lead in the future. Be specific about identifying a particular group or class that will be the focus for your practice exercises throughout this workbook. At the end of each chapter is a checklist that may be used by individual group leaders as a self-assessment tool to assess their own group process skills, and it may be used by supervisors as an evaluation tool.

This group process book is designed for several purposes of use. Individual practitioners and peer leaders may use the workbook on their own to improve their skills in leading groups and classes. Individuals who are new to leading groups may read through the guidelines and practice exercises as a way to teach themselves the skills in facilitating a group or class. In addition, experienced group leaders may want a refresher of some of the guidelines of group process. This workbook also is designed as a teaching tool for program directors and supervisors to use in training staff how to facilitate a group in their agencies as well as for instructors to use in academic settings when teaching the concepts of group process.

As more and more peer specialists and consumer-providers are leading and co-leading groups and classes, there is a separate chapter included in this book specifically for promoting peer leadership. While the general group process guidelines are the same for anyone leading a group or class, the chapter on promoting peer leadership discusses some of the unique and valuable contributions that peers can add to a group or class, such as self-disclosing experiences and how to incorporate those relevant experiences into the group or class content. Peers provide a very important role in leading and co-leading groups and classes because peers can engage and

© 2009, Trustees of Boston University. All rights reserved. Center for Psychiatric Rehabilitation.

relate to the other group members in an exceptional way that is helpful and inspirational to others.

Many of the suggestions and tips included in these group process guidelines were derived from our Center's *Psychiatric Rehabilitation Training Technology* (Cohen, Danley, & Nemec, 1985, 2007; Cohen, Farkas, & Cohen, 1986, 2007; Cohen, Farkas, Cohen, & Unger, 1991, 2007; Cohen, Nemec, & Farkas, 2000), *Case Management Training Technology* (Cohen, Nemec, Farkas, Forbess, & Cohen, 1988), the *Leader's Guide—The Recovery Workbook: Practical Coping and Empowerment Strategies for People with Psychiatric Disabilities* (1994); as well as years of experience from the authors' work in leading groups and classes.

We would like to acknowledge and thank all of the people we have worked with in groups and classes as well as our own teachers and mentors over the years. Our students and group participants have provided us with inspiration, and our mentors have been our role models and have provided us guidance about what works well with group process. We also would like to acknowledge and thank Bill Anthony, our group leader and mentor, for his encouragement to develop this book; Kathy Furlong-Norman for her endorsement of this publication; and Linda Getgen for her continuous support and for her creativity in designing and publishing this book.

Best wishes as you learn about the group process guidelines and the skills of becoming an effective group leader.

Chapter 1: Planning for the Group Activity

1.1	Identifying the Group Structure and Roles
1.2	Identifying the Group Participants
1.3	Identifying the Group Objectives
1.4	Organizing the Activity Materials
1.5	Preparing Yourself
1.6	Arranging the Environment
Checklist:	Planning for the Group Activity

Chapter 1: Planning for the Group Activity

Planning for the group activity is done *before* the group activity is held. Planning for the group or class ahead of time is extremely important and can be one of the best things a leader can do to be well organized and ready for the group. Planning for the group activity prepares you as the leader to conduct the group with consideration and forethought. Once you are well prepared and organized, then you will be freed up to pay full attention to the participants *during* the group activity. Planning for the group activity involves a series of preparation skills:

1.1   Identifying the Group Structure and Roles

1.2   Identifying the Group Participants

1.3   Identifying the Group Objectives

1.4   Organizing the Activity Materials

1.5   Preparing Yourself

1.6   Arranging the Environment

Each one of these preparation skills will be discussed with explanations and suggestions along with examples and practices sprinkled throughout this chapter.

1.1 Identifying the Group Structure and Roles

Identifying the group structure and roles is setting up the organization of the group and the roles of the group members when preparing for the group. It gets you started in thinking seriously about the group composition and how it will be run. Here are some tips you can use when identifying the group structure and roles:

- **Frame the group experience as educational.** Group leaders should communicate clearly to participants that they will be involved in an educational experience and that they will be students in this group. Although many people with psychiatric disabilities have been involved in different therapeutic groups, the role of being a student can be an important and healthy aspect of a person's developing sense of self. It shifts the focus away from other identities that can be stigmatizing and debilitating for many people, such as patient or client.

- **Clarify the role of the student when preparing for the class or group.** Identify whether this is a new role for participants at your agency or one that is familiar to them. Think about what kinds of expectations you have in mind for the students for your particular class. For example:
    — Is this a class where you want students to actively participate in discussions?
    — Will students be expected to take notes?
    — Will students have some type of homework assignments?

For your next class or group activity, list the expectations for the students:

Group Participant's Role	Participation Expectations

- **Record** the name of the activity, the purpose of the activity, and any expectations of the participants on a chalkboard or flipchart sheet and posting the sheet on the activity room wall before each session.
- **Collaborate with others during the teaching or group process,** such as staff or program administrators. Such collaboration often is required by the setting of the teaching. Depending on the setting where teaching occurs, educational group leaders may be required to share information about group discussions or group members with others, such as a group member's primary clinician. Collaborating with mental health agency staff and administrators is an important role for the group leader, who will need to clarify in advance what sorts of coordination and information sharing will be required.

For your next group activity, who might you need to collaborate with and why?

Name of Person	Their Role

© 2009, Trustees of Boston University. All rights reserved. Center for Psychiatric Rehabilitation.

- **Address confidentiality issues** because of this potential need to share information with others and to provide a safe teaching environment. It is useful to identify in advance specifically what type of information will be shared and with whom. When the leader explains and values the need for collaboration with other key people, group members are more likely to agree to sharing information with the staff.

    What type of information might you need to share with others for your next group?

Name of Person	Type of Information to Share

- **Discuss rules about confidentiality among the group members.** Confidentiality acknowledges the students' natural need to discuss their experiences in the class, but prevents revealing the names of those participating or identifying personal information shared by class participants.

    What are your agency's policies about confidentiality?

- **Clarify the roles of the leaders.** Sometimes there is more than one leader in the group or class. This can be very helpful in sharing teaching duties and in supporting one another. It is important that one leader has the major responsibility at any given time. As a co-teacher, it is helpful to meet before the class and to identify ahead of time when one teacher will be the primary leader for each class session. The teacher, who is not the primary leader at a particular time, can observe the class and the ongoing group process. Make it clear when primary leader roles are changing because it may not be obvious to the students.

Do you typically co-lead groups? ☐ Yes ☐ No

What has happened when you have facilitated a group with another leader?

_____
_____
_____
_____
_____
_____
_____
_____

For programs that use *The Recovery Workbook (Spaniol, Koehler, & Hutchinson, 1994, 2009)*, it is suggested that groups should be co-led by a professional and a consumer. This balance of perspectives and experiences helps the facilitation of the recovery group. The leaders support each other and provide feedback to each other during planning meetings and supervision meetings.

Similarly, many family education and family support groups are co-led by a staff person and a family member. Each leader contributes valuable information and experiences to these groups.

Some teachers may be mental health professionals, who also are family members or mental health consumers. The role the teacher takes in these instances would depend on the nature of the learning experience. For example, if the class is taught ordinarily by peers, then the teacher should stay in the role of a peer and not in the role of a professional. This can be accomplished by sticking with the curriculum and commenting from one's own personal experience rather than from one's professional experience. Staying with your own personal experience will connect you to the students as a peer rather than as the "expert." It also will help to build students' confidence in recognizing their own expertise and in coming up with their own solutions.

What experiences have you had co-leading groups with family members and/or mental health consumers?

_____
_____
_____
_____
_____
_____

If you are a peer leader, how do you distinguish between your personal role and your professional role?

_____
_____
_____
_____
_____
_____

- **Identify boundaries in the group.** An initial agreement helps establish boundaries in the class. The agreements made at the start of the classes are primarily a commitment people make to themselves. They have chosen to take the class because they hope it will meet their needs. It is an opportunity for them to begin, continue, and successfully complete something for themselves. When someone joins the class, they also are making a commitment to the other students and to the teacher. It can be useful to articulate the terms of the agreement. Such an agreement may cover the following points:

  — Agree to be present each week, to be on time, and to remain throughout the entire class.

  — Agree to work actively on the information, skill, and support needs that brought me to the class.

  — Agree to put my feelings into words, not into actions.

  — Agree to continue participation until the final class.

  — Agree to protect the names, identities, and personal information of my fellow group members when discussing what has happened in the class.

  — Agree to limit comments in class to two minutes.

© 2009, Trustees of Boston University. All rights reserved. Center for Psychiatric Rehabilitation.

What additional items might you add to your agreement for your next group or class?

_____
_____
_____
_____
_____
_____
_____

- **Address consequences when someone doesn't meet the expectations of the group or class or doesn't meet the demands of the role as a group member.** How will you decide if someone is no longer considered a member of the group? It usually is best to air on the side of leniency and allowing people to stay in the group, unless there is a formal exit process.

    How do you address is the issue of unmet expectations at your agency or program?

    _____
    _____
    _____
    _____
    _____
    _____
    _____

- Finally, be sure to **inform participants and any relevant others in advance about the group meeting time and place.** It is best to put the meeting time and place in writing, such as an e-mail notice or posted on a bulletin board in a common area.

© 2009, Trustees of Boston University. All rights reserved. Center for Psychiatric Rehabilitation.

1.2 Identifying the Group Participants

Identifying the Group Participants means creating a list of people who will be involved in your group activity. It helps to think about the group members ahead of time in order to prepare yourself for how to address various participants. There are several factors to consider when identifying group members.

- **Decide on the number of group members for your activity.** The size of the group can be based on the topic, the physical space, agency requirements, etc. Some groups that are more educational in nature can withstand larger numbers of people, while other groups that are more intimate in nature and discussion oriented may work better with smaller numbers.

    How many participants are typically in your groups or classes at your agency?

    Number of Participants   *Type of Group or Class*

    _____   _____
    _____   _____
    _____   _____
    _____   _____
    _____   _____
    _____   _____
    _____   _____

    What factors at your agency contribute to the size of your groups or classes?

    _____
    _____
    _____
    _____
    _____

- **Identify who might need to be involved in your group activity based on the topic of the group.** Assess how the topic may relate to the individuals' interest in the content, their goals, and their specific learning needs.

    For your next group, identify who might be involved. Identify how the group might be helpful to each person and why each person might be additive to the group.

Names of Participants	How the group will be helpful?	How will the participant be additive to the group?

- **Consider the participants' composition as a group.** Decide whether it might be better to have a homogeneous group, where people have very similar goals and learning needs vs. a heterogeneous group, where people are very diverse in many ways.

    In your experience, which type of group works best for you as a group leader—a homogeneous group or heterogeneous group and why?

    ☐ Homogeneous group ☐ Heterogeneous group

© 2009, Trustees of Boston University. All rights reserved. Center for Psychiatric Rehabilitation.

- **Assess the pace of the students in the class.** Are they typically fast learners or slow learners? Generally most groups will have a typical bell curve of learning paces. A couple of people may be very fast learners, a couple of people may be very slow at learning, and the majority of the group members fall in the middle. Consider employing a tutoring approach where the faster learners or teaching assistants help out the slower learners in the group.

    Based on your knowledge of the group members you listed for your group or class, assess the pace of the learners.

Names of Group Members	Fast	Average	Slow
_____	☐	☐	☐
_____	☐	☐	☐
_____	☐	☐	☐
_____	☐	☐	☐
_____	☐	☐	☐
_____	☐	☐	☐
_____	☐	☐	☐
_____	☐	☐	☐
_____	☐	☐	☐
_____	☐	☐	☐

- **Pay attention to the individual learning styles of the group members.** There are a couple of different types of learning styles:
    — Auditory, which is learning best by listening to lectures and instructions.
    — Visual, which is learning best by seeing examples and demonstrations.
    — Experiential, which is learning best by doing. Most people are experiential learners when a skill is being taught. Most people need to be able to practice the skill being taught.

    However, there usually is a split between auditory learners and visual learners. It's helpful to be aware of the individuals' learning styles when preparing your group materials. More lecture points explanations are needed for auditory learners, while more examples and written instructions are needed for visual learners.

    What type of learner are you? ☐ Auditory ☐ Visual

    Sometimes it's harder to break out of your own learning mode in order to teach to people in the other learning mode. However, it is critical to think about the learning differences and to plan for a variety of teaching methods.

Based on your knowledge of the group members on your list, identify who might be an auditory learner vs. a visual learner.

Names of Group Members	Auditory	Visual
_____	☐	☐
_____	☐	☐
_____	☐	☐
_____	☐	☐
_____	☐	☐
_____	☐	☐
_____	☐	☐
_____	☐	☐
_____	☐	☐

There also are different modes of learning:

— Abstract, which is more conceptual in style. Abstract learners like to talk about the philosophy, the principles, and the meaning behind what is being taught.

— Concrete, which is more tangible and practical in style. Concrete learners like to know the specific steps and procedures for what is to be done.

What type of learner are you? ☐ Abstract ☐ Concrete

Based on your knowledge of the group members on your list, identify who might be an abstract learner vs. a concrete learner.

Names of Group Members	Abstract	Concrete
_____	☐	☐
_____	☐	☐
_____	☐	☐
_____	☐	☐
_____	☐	☐
_____	☐	☐
_____	☐	☐
_____	☐	☐
_____	☐	☐

© 2009, Trustees of Boston University. All rights reserved. Center for Psychiatric Rehabilitation.

1.3 Identifying the Group Objectives

Identifying the Group Objectives means listing what the individuals will learn or gain from participating in the group or class. Identifying the group objectives helps the leader to develop a purpose and guidelines for the group's content.

- **Create objectives that are obvious results from taking part in a group or class.** Objectives should not be grandiose promises. Instead, objectives should be direct outcomes from satisfactory group participation. Some examples of objectives are:
    - Participants will be able to identify examples of feeling words and their intensities.
    - Participants will be able to discriminate the difference between an open-ended question and a closed question.

- **Write objectives clearly using specific behavioral terms that are actions that can be seen or heard,** for instance:
    - Participants will be able to list…
    - Participants will be able to recite…
    - Participants will be able to outline…

    Objectives should not have vague terms like, "learn" or "understand."

    Name some verbs that are observable actions that can be seen or heard by others.

    _____
    _____
    _____
    _____

- **Identify only 2 or 3 objectives for each group session or class.** You don't want to promise the world as a result of your group or class! Listing only a couple of objectives will limit the content of what you plan to cover in the group session or teach in the class, and they will provide the leader with a focus and specific purpose for that session.

    _____
    _____
    _____
    _____

List a couple of objectives for your upcoming group or class.

_____
_____
_____
_____
_____
_____
_____

1.4 Organizing the Activity Materials

Organizing the Activity Materials means to gather the materials needed for the group activity. Organizing the activity materials ensures that you will have what you need in order to lead the group activity. The more organized you can be with your materials, the easier it will be for the group members to be involved and participating actively. Organizing the activity materials involves:

- **Create an activity schedule** for the classes or groups that have multiple sessions. Divide the material up into manageable parts to match your group's objectives and allotted time.

    How many sessions might you need for your group or class?

    Will you need a: ☐ one-time session?   ☐ multiple sessions?

    If multiple sessions, how many? _____

    How much time will you need for each session? _____

    How many sessions will you hold per week? _____

- **Keep the schedule loose enough to allow for group discussions and for sharing experiences and thoughts about the activity content.** Remember when creating the schedule to make adjustments for any holidays or vacation plans.

- **Use a variety of types of materials to add interest to the group activity.** Take into account the participants' learning styles—auditory or visual. Depending on the activity, materials may include: handouts, lesson plans or activity descriptions, flipchart sheets, worksheets, pens/pencils, and computer or audiovisual equipment. Design new materials, use current materials, and/or modify current materials. If you're planning to use existing materials for an activity, be certain that the material is tailored to the preferences and abilities of the group members.

© 2009, Trustees of Boston University. All rights reserved. Center for Psychiatric Rehabilitation.

Based on the topic of your group or class, what are some examples of materials you might use?

_____
_____
_____
_____
_____
_____

- **Photocopy any handouts to outline or illustrate major points of the discussion.** Be sure to put page numbers on handouts in a packet or booklet.

    What are some examples of handouts you might use for your group or class?

    _____
    _____
    _____
    _____
    _____
    _____

- **Supply each group participant with a folder or a notebook to record and organize handouts and materials used in the activity.** Distribute the material for each session either before the session begins or as soon as possible once the group starts.

- **Plan examples to illustrate or demonstrate any skills that are to be taught.** Examples may include cartoons, scenarios, role-plays, or demonstrations. Pick the type of example that best shows what is being taught. Examples may show the end product of a task, or they may show the process of how the task is performed. For instance, for the skill of washing clothes, you might want to demonstrate the steps of sorting the clothes, loading the machine, and starting the machine. For the skill of scheduling leisure time, you might want to show a completed calendar filled with events and activities.

On the next few pages are some illustrations of different types of examples. There are a couple of photographs for a physical skill of Deep Breathing, a role-play for an emotional skill of Expressing Feelings, and an outline for an intellectual skill of Identifying Key Points.

Example: Instructions and Photographs for the Skill of Deep Breathing

While sitting or standing, keep your back erect.

Inhale deeply and hold the breath for a few counts.

Slowly exhale and relax.

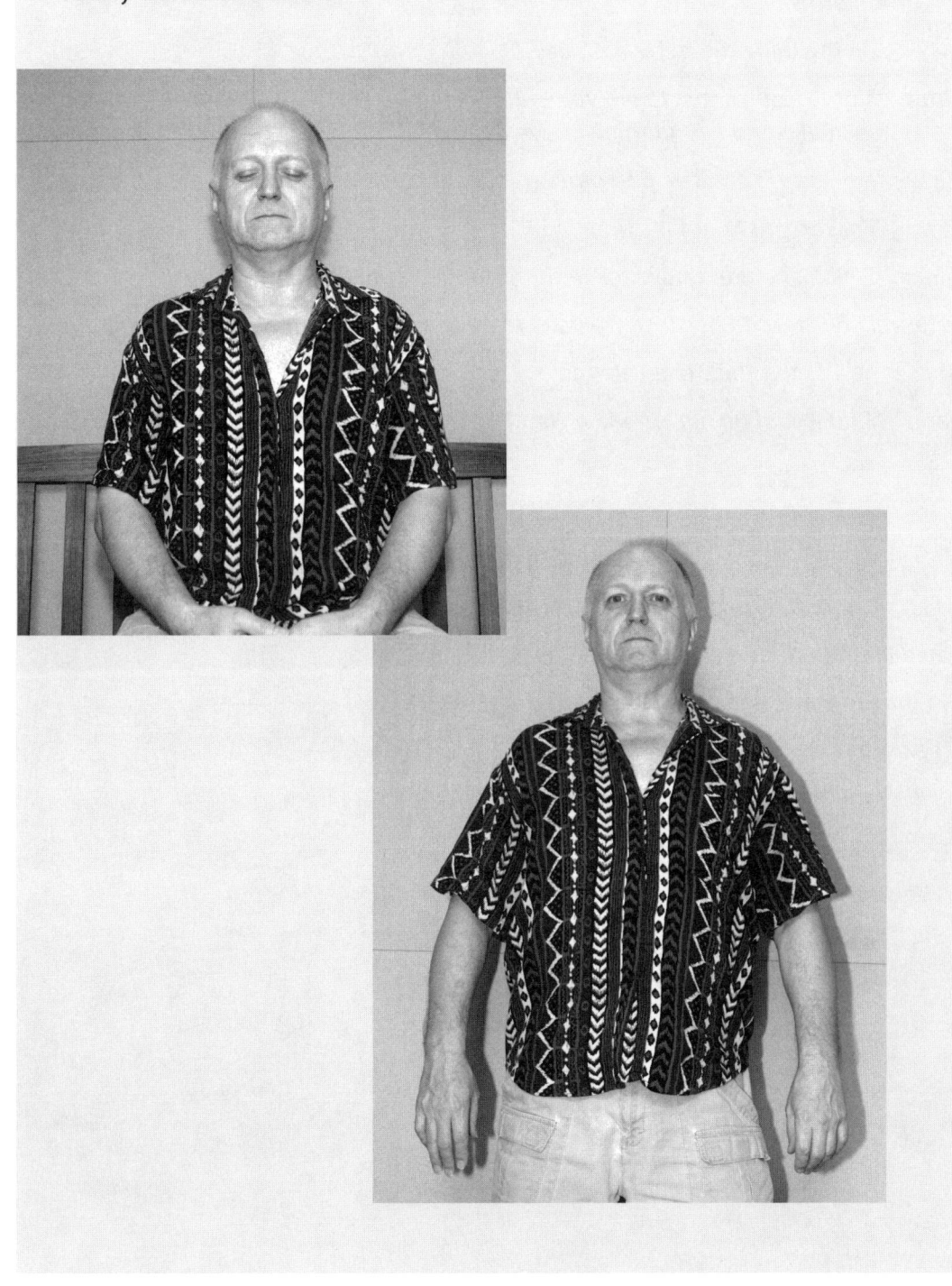

© 2009, Trustees of Boston University. All rights reserved. Center for Psychiatric Rehabilitation.

Example of a Role-Play for the skill of Expressing Feelings

Sara: *(Yawning). I haven't slept well in three days. I wonder what's bothering me? It must be Tina, my coworker. She has been snapping at me lately, and it's been very upsetting.*

How am I feeling? Sad? Depressed? Rejected? Angry? I think I'm feeling two things—I feel angry because I haven't done anything to deserve her snipes. And I feel sad because Tina used to be fun to work with.

I wonder if I should tell her. What would she say if I did? Maybe I'll tell her tomorrow.

...in the lunchroom the next day...

Sara: *"Tina, I just wanted to tell you that I feel upset because you've been snapping at me lately, and I don't think I have done anything to deserve it."*

Tina: *"I'm sorry, Sara. I've had other things on my mind lately."*

Sara: *"I'm sorry to hear that Tina."*

Tina: *"Well, I shouldn't have taken things out on you."*

Sara: *"I just feel sad because we used to have a lot of fun times working together."*

Tina: *"Yes, I miss that, too. Let's go out for lunch tomorrow?"*

Sara: *"That would be fun. Thanks, Tina."*

Example of an Outline for the Skill of Identifying Key Points

When preparing for a class or lesson:

I. Choose Main Idea or Discussion Topic

　A. Consider topic from a series

　B. Pick high priority topic

II. Distinguish Important Points of Topic

　A. List relevant points

　B. Select points in order of importance

　C. List points in sequential order

III. Expand on Important Points

　A. Give verbal examples of points, i.e., stories and explanations

　B. Create illustrations of points

What kinds of examples might you use for your group or class?

_____

Plan one example for your group or class on the next page. Be sure to plan it thoroughly with dialogue, pictures, or specific instructions for a demonstration.

Example for your next group or class

- **Create practice exercises and activities ahead of time.** Make sure that you have written out clear instructions for what the participants specifically are supposed to do for the exercise. If the exercise is written, then the directions should be written on the worksheet. Include any worksheets or materials that might be needed for the practice.

Listed below and on the next page are some illustrations of different types of practice exercises. These practice exercises continue with the skills of Deep Breathing, Expressing Feelings, and Identifying Key Points.

Practice Exercise for the skill of Deep Breathing

Instructions:
For this exercise, I'd like you to practice the skill of Deep Breathing first while sitting in a chair. Be sure to keep your back erect, inhale deeply, and hold the breath for a few counts; then slowly exhale and relax.

Now repeat steps of Deep Breathing for this practice while standing.

Practice Exercise for the skill of Expressing Feelings

Instructions:
Listen to the following situation and Express your Feelings to Joe or Jane (our volunteer, who is role-playing as your roommate). For this practice, you may talk through all the steps out loud. Remember that the steps for the skill of Expressing Feelings are: Identify the Feeling, Choose When to Share, and State the Feeling.

Scenario:
Your roommate just came home drunk at 3:00 in the morning for the third day in a row.

© 2009, Trustees of Boston University. All rights reserved. Center for Psychiatric Rehabilitation.

Practice Exercise for the skill of Identifying Key Points

Instructions:
Use the worksheet below to Identify Key Points for your next class or lesson. Remember to choose the main idea or discussion topic, distinguish important points of topic, and expand on important points.

I. _____

    A. _____

    B. _____

    C. _____

    D. _____

    E. _____

II. _____

    A. _____

    B. _____

    C. _____

    D. _____

    E. _____

III. _____

    A. _____

    B. _____

    C. _____

    D. _____

    E. _____

What kinds of practice exercises might you use for your group or class?

_____
_____
_____
_____
_____
_____
_____
_____
_____
_____
_____
_____
_____
_____
_____
_____
_____
_____

Plan one exercise for your next group or class and write out the instructions on the next page. Use the same group or class topic as the one you used when you designed an example on page 20. Be sure to include specific instructions and any worksheets or props, as needed.

© 2009, Trustees of Boston University. All rights reserved. Center for Psychiatric Rehabilitation.

Practice Exercise for your next group or class
Instructions:

1.5 Preparing Yourself

Preparing Yourself means readying your mind and body to engage fully in the group activity. Preparing yourself promotes your ability to concentrate in the moment and to give full attention to your group participants. Preparing yourself involves:

- **Grooming and dressing appropriately for the group activity.** Since much of the focus of a group is drawn towards the group leader, your appearance needs to be appealing, but not distracting in any way from the content of the group. A group leader needs to avoid wearing clothes that might provoke any external distractions, such as wearing revealing clothing, e.g., short skirts, pants that ride too low off hips, midriff tops, or low-cut tops; or T-shirts or buttons with slogans that could be offensive to some group members or that might divert attention away from the group's content. The leader's physical appearance should be clean and well-kempt.

  The leader's clothes should match the type of group activity. For example, if the group is in a professional atmosphere, such as a conference or a meeting, then your attire may need to be more formal. Conversely, if the group is more informal in nature or a physical activity, then your attire should be more casual. The attention of the participants should be on the activity or the content of the group, rather than on any inappropriate appearance of the leader.

  What would you wear if you were leading:

  — a staff training on communication skills _____

  — a cooking class_____

  — a family group meeting _____

  — a skill lesson on writing a resumé _____

  — a skill lesson on washing clothes _____

- **Eliminating internal distractions** is very important to do before starting a group session or activity. Examples of internal distractions may be thoughts about something other than the group or its members, such as what to cook for dinner that night or replaying a conversation in your mind that you had with a friend from the night before. Depending on what you've been thinking about, eliminating internal distractions may take just a minute or may take a longer, more concerted effort. Some techniques for eliminating internal distractions might include:

  — Practice relaxation/centering techniques, such as deep breathing or yoga exercises.

    What types of relaxation techniques work best for you?

    _____

    _____

    _____

    _____

© 2009, Trustees of Boston University. All rights reserved. Center for Psychiatric Rehabilitation.

— Physical self-care and comfort, such as taking a walk around the block or putting your feet up before a group activity.

What types of self-care techniques help you?

_____
_____
_____
_____

— Focus on the activity and the group members rather than on yourself. Focusing on others also may reduce a leader's own anxiety about teaching a group.

— Use positive self-talk to reduce nervousness and improve confidence. For example, you may remind yourself that you know the content well and probably better than any of the group members. Remind yourself that you are the leader of the group and can positively affect how the group is run.

What positive self-talk messages would you typically say to yourself?

_____
_____
_____
_____

— Review the materials right before the group activity. It's important to be well-acquainted with the content of the group, even if you've taught the class many times before. The more organized you are in your own mind with the content as well as with the materials, the smoother the group should run.

— Anticipate a challenging piece—don't avoid it, and get support for it, if needed.

What is an example of a challenge you might anticipate for yourself when leading a group activity?

_____
_____
_____
_____

1.6 Arranging the Environment

Arranging the Environment means structuring the physical setting to promote learning. Arranging the environment creates a supportive learning atmosphere. You will want the participants to pay attention to you and the content of the group activity, rather than any extraneous distractions in the environment. Arranging the environment involves a couple of steps:

- **Organize the room to maximize opportunities for engagement.** Before beginning each activity session, arrange the room to ensure as relaxed an environment as possible with minimal distractions. Attend to the comfort and accessibility of the room for the group participants.

    — For group discussions, arrange chairs and tables in a "U" shape with the chairs outside of the tables, or ensure that the chairs and tables are arranged so that the instructor can have direct eye contact with as many participants as possible without the need to move, and so that as many participants as possible are able to have eye contact with each other.

    — Select chairs that are comfortable, but not too comfortable because people may feel too relaxed and sleepy.

    — Allow space for anyone needing wheelchair accessibility. Leaving a space at the end of a table or row of chairs makes access easier.

    — Use a chalkboard or post flipchart sheets where participants have direct visual access. Consider posting signs, pictures, and/or posters that offer encouraging and inspiring messages related to the group activity.

    For your next group activity, describe the room or physical space will you be using.

    _____
    _____
    _____
    _____
    _____
    _____

    Practice arranging the environment by organizing the room where you will hold your group or class.

© 2009, Trustees of Boston University. All rights reserved. Center for Psychiatric Rehabilitation.

- **Eliminate external distractions in the room, such as temperature, noise, and lights.**
  — People vary in their comfort regarding the temperature of the room because invariably some will think it's too hot and some will think it's too cold. If possible, try to adjust the thermostat to a medium temperature or even slightly cooler. The larger the group of people, the warmer the room will feel, despite the thermostat setting. If the temperature is too warm, people may tend to get sleepy, while cooler temperatures tend to help people feel more alert.

  — Shut any windows if there is noise outside, like traffic or construction. Turn off any radios or TVs in the room that are not being used as part of the activity.

  — Adjust the lights in the room so that they are bright enough to keep participants alert and focused. If PowerPoint slides or videos are used for an activity, you may lower the lights, but remember to turn them back on as soon as you have finished using that equipment.

  — Attend to the cleanliness and clutter in order to create an organized learning environment. Too many posters on a wall may be a distraction, unless they pertain to the content of the group activity. Keep the area clean and well-organized to promote attentiveness.

  — Clean off the chalkboard or whiteboard and/or remove any flipchart pages after particular content points have been made. Old content information can be distracting once you've moved onto discussing a new topic.

  What distractions does your group room or activity space have?

  _____
  _____
  _____
  _____
  _____
  _____

  Practice arranging the environment by eliminating distractions in the room where you will hold your group or class.

This concludes the section on Planning for the Group Activity. You may use the checklist on the next page to assess your own skills when planning for your next group or class. In addition, your supervisor may use the checklist to evaluate your group preparation skills.

CHECKLIST: Planning for the Group Activity

Name of Group Leader: _____

Name of Group Activity: _____ Date _____

Identified the Group Structure and Roles	☐ Yes	☐ No	☐ Partial

Comments _____

_____

Identified the Group Participants	☐ Yes	☐ No	☐ Partial

Comments _____

_____

Identified the Group Objectives	☐ Yes	☐ No	☐ Partial

Comments _____

_____

Organized the Activity Materials	☐ Yes	☐ No	☐ Partial

Comments _____

_____

Prepared Yourself	☐ Yes	☐ No	☐ Partial

Comments _____

_____

Arranged the Environment	☐ Yes	☐ No	☐ Partial

Comments _____

_____

© 2009, Trustees of Boston University. All rights reserved. Center for Psychiatric Rehabilitation.

Chapter 2: Conducting the Group Activity

2.1	Reviewing the Group Structure and Roles
2.2	Reviewing the Group Objectives
2.3	Orienting to the Activity
2.4	Giving Directions
2.5	Presenting the Activity Content
2.6	Presenting to Individuals within a Group
2.7	Modifying the Content and/or Pace
2.8	Summarizing the Group Activity
Checklist:	Conducting the Group Activity

Chapter 2: Conducting the Group Activity

Conducting the group activity is done *during* the group activity. Conducting the group activity involves a set of skills that the leader or teacher performs to facilitate the group or class. Conducting the group activity takes practice and experience to ensure a smooth delivery of content and facilitation of the group. Conducting the group activity involves a series of skills:

2.1   Reviewing the Group Structure and Roles

2.2   Reviewing the Group Objectives

2.3   Orienting to the Activity

2.4   Giving Directions

2.5   Presenting the Activity Content

2.6   Presenting to Individuals within a Group

2.7   Modifying the Content and/or Pace

2.8   Summarizing the Group Activity

Each one of these skills for conducting the group activity will be discussed with explanations and suggestions along with examples and practices throughout this chapter.

2.1 Reviewing the Group Structure and Roles

*Reviewing the Group Structure and Role*s is discussing the organization of the group and the roles of the group members when starting the group activity or class. Reviewing the group structure and roles is one of the first things covered in the first group session. Reviewing the group structure and roles allows you to talk about the group composition and how it will be run. It paves the way to set the ground rules before getting started with the content of the class or activity. When reviewing the group structure and roles, here are a few suggestions:

- **Explain things as clearly as possible** when orienting to the class schedule. While you've created the schedule in preparation for the class, be flexible to make changes, if needed.

- **Hand out a written copy of the class schedule, the group expectations, and any other main points to each group member.** Many people need the visual list as well as the verbal instructions. The visual aspect reinforces the points discussed in class and can be referred to later, if reminders are needed.

- **Discuss the behavioral expectations for the group at the beginning of the first session.** Be aware that sometimes you will need to repeat the behavioral expectations periodically.

- **Allow time at the beginning of each class for general announcements about special events, procedural changes, and/or schedule changes.** This allows time for participants to process what is happening and to deal with any feelings about the class before you start in on the content of the class. It usually is better to inform people of announcements at the beginning of the class, rather than at the end, so that you have time to answer any questions and to respond to any concerns.

© 2009, Trustees of Boston University. All rights reserved. Center for Psychiatric Rehabilitation.

- **Allow time for people to attend to their own needs** for:
  - breaks
  - medication issues
  - time for participants to talk with the leader privately before or after a group, when needed

2.2 Reviewing the Group Objectives

Reviewing the Group Objectives means discussing what the individuals will learn or gain from participating in the group activity or class. Reviewing the group objectives allows the leader to share the purpose and guidelines for the group's content. In order to be very clear, you may want to write the group objectives on the chalkboard or flipchart and/or hand out a written copy to each of the group members.

2.3 Orienting to the Activity

Orienting to the Activity means giving information about an upcoming activity. Orienting gives the participants a preview of the activities. Orienting involves people in what's about to happen. An orientation explains what will happen, why it will happen, what the group leader will do, and what the participants are expected to do. Orienting to the activity involves:

- **Describe briefly what the activity is,** similar to a definition.

- **Discuss the intended benefits of the class,** which helps to provide the group members with some reasons to participate in the activity.

- **Explain the expectations and roles of each participant and the group leader,** which helps people understand how to contribute to the group.

- **Review the participants' understanding before beginning the activity** to make sure that you are ready to start. After Orienting, the leader determines whether the participants have understood the orientation. If they are not sure what was said, then you need to reorient the participants, using fresh words to explain the upcoming activity.

On the next page is an example of an orientation.

Example of Orienting
- **Activity Description:**
  "Today we're going to begin a series of classes on communication and friendship skills. Before we get started, I'd like to take a couple of minutes to orient you to what we're going to do.

  There are many skills involved to improve your ability to communicate and to enrich your friendships. In this series of social skills classes, we will discuss six important skills: Initiating Conversations, Extending Invitations, Offering Assistance, Recognizing Conflict Situations, Expressing Feelings, and Apologizing. We will take a couple of class sessions for each of the skills."

  Ask: *"What questions do you have about what I have explained?"*

  Respond to answers.

- **Activity Benefits:**

  Ask: *"How might this series of social skills classes be helpful to you?"*

  Respond to answers.

- **Roles and Expectations:**
  "As the instructor, I will tell you some information about each skill, show you some examples, and give you some practice exercises along with some feedback of how you performed each of the skills. As a group member, I'd like you to ask any questions about the skill lessons, answer any questions that I pose during the class, and participate in the practice exercises."

  Ask: *"Just so I know that I have been clear, please tell me in your own words what I am asking you to do before we begin this first class of social skills."*

  Respond to answers.

- **Orienting occurs at the beginning of each activity, when an activity has been interrupted, or as often as necessary.** Reorientation is needed when participants seem confused or distracted from the task. Sometimes reorienting is helpful when the leader or group members veer off topic in discussion. Reorienting allows people to refocus on the group activity.
- **When group sessions continue as a series, it is important to review the prior session with participants before starting a new session.** Ask participants to recall learning points from prior sessions as well as and their experiences with it.
- In addition, it may be helpful to orient people again to the process of the group.

On the next page is a practice worksheet for orienting. Read the directions and write an orientation for your next group or activity. Feel free to use the example above as a guide.

© 2009, Trustees of Boston University. All rights reserved. Center for Psychiatric Rehabilitation.

Practice for Orienting

Directions:

Write an orientation for new group you are leading. Write word-for-word what you would say to the group participants to orient them to the activity.

- Activity Description:

_____
_____
_____
_____
_____

- Activity Benefits:

_____
_____
_____
_____
_____

- Roles and Expectations:

_____
_____
_____
_____
_____

2.4 Giving Directions

Giving Directions means telling the group participants what to do during an activity. Giving directions clarifies the specific instructions that the leader has for the group members to participate in the activity. Directions may include a step-by-step procedure to follow, and they may be verbal or written. When giving directions:

- **Break down the task or activity into specific steps.** Directions often are needed before showing an example or beginning a practice exercise.

- **Explain clearly what the participants are expected to do.** When explaining to participants what you want them to do during the activity, specifically describe the desired behavior. For example, *"Now I'd like each of you to think of at least one thing you have learned in today's group, and tell me what it is when I ask you."*

    Avoid using terms that may be vague or may not be understood in the same way by each person, such as, *"What did you get out of today's group?"*

- **Direct individuals to pay attention to you when giving directions,** such as, *"I'd like everyone to look at me, make eye contact, and listen carefully to my instructions for this next practice."*

- **Stand in front of the group making sweeping eye contact when giving directions,** but at times it may be necessary to move closer to a particular individual in order to establish or maintain his or her attention.

- **Speak in a clear, measured, and loud enough voice** to get the attention of the participants when giving directions.

    Write out some directions that you would use in your next class or group activity.

© 2009, Trustees of Boston University. All rights reserved. Center for Psychiatric Rehabilitation.

2.5 Presenting the Activity Content

Presenting the Activity Content means sharing new knowledge about a topic, skill, or activity. Presenting the activity content transfers your knowledge and skills to the group participants. Presenting the activity content involves three main techniques:

- **Tell information about the topic, skill, or activity.**
  - Generally, information is shared verbally, but it also may be presented in writing, such as an outline of procedures or a list of steps.
  - Present content information in different ways, using fun facts, helpful hints, timely tips, and clever clarifications!
  - Show a passion and enthusiasm for the subject you're talking about—it engages people more.
  - Repeat information in different ways and with different words to reinforce your message. People may not always understand something the first time you say it, but it may become clearer after a second explanation with different words.

- **Show examples for participants to see how a skill is performed or what an activity should look like.** Using visual aids and showing examples illustrates lecture points for the content. Examples keep a lesson interesting, and they are especially helpful for visual learners.

  As discussed in chapter 1, examples may show the end product of a task, or they may show the process of how the task is performed. It is very important to make sure that your examples are accurate representations of the skill or task. A poor example may leave a lasting bad impression. Often it is helpful to have more than one example prepared to give another image of a task or skill performance.

- **Facilitate exercises to give participants a chance to practice the skill or task.** Since most people learn best by doing or performing a skill, practices are critical to reinforce what has been told and shown. Practice exercises keep participants involved and interactive. In addition to offering group members a chance to practice, each person is given feedback on his or her performance of the task or skill. Information about feedback will be discussed in chapter 3, in section 3.10 Critiquing Participation and Progress.

2.6 Presenting to Individuals within a Group

Presenting to Individuals within a Group means identifying how you will explain information to a group and to each individual within a group. When presenting the activity content to a group of participants, be sure to communicate the information generically to the group. In other words, explain the facts and show the examples to the entire group. However, it is important to personalize the information to the individuals within the group whenever possible. Each individual may have a different reason for attending the class or learning the skill, and each individual may have a different way that he or she will use the information in his or her life. For example, you may have a group of people who are learning the skill of interviewing for a job. The basic steps of interviewing would be the same for anyone and would be taught to the group. However, each participant may be interviewing for different jobs, and it would be important to talk to each individual about how they could tailor their job interview to highlight their particular strengths for that particular job. Therefore, it is important to remember that when teaching in a group, to teach the concepts generically and then to personalize the information for each individual's circumstances.

What are some examples of how you would personalize information to individuals within your group or class?

Names of Participants   *Personalized Information*

_____   _____

_____   _____

_____   _____

_____   _____

_____   _____

_____   _____

_____   _____

2.7 Modifying the Content and/or Pace

Modifying the Content and/or Pace means adjusting the information and the speed with which you present different components of the activity based on the response or reactions of your group participants. Modifying the content and/or pace increases the comfort and openness of the learners to acquire new knowledge and skills.

- **Assess the participants' engagement in the group activity.** Watch for body language and facial expressions to gauge interest and involvement. Watch for how the pace can affect the group to be faster or slower. Group behavior can be contagious. Group members sometimes may give input or make decisions about the pace of learning, so feel free to ask participants how the group is going for them.

- **Review the participants' acquisition of knowledge and skills.** Some content may provoke more self-disclosures and experiential talks. You may need to modify the pace to allow for the time for a full discussion.

- **Adjust your schedule to meet the needs of the learners.** Most groups will have a natural bell curve of participation. Some members will lag behind, while others will speed ahead. You may ask the speedy learners to help others who are having trouble. Modify the pace to match the speed of the majority of the group in the bell curve. You may need to connect with people who are having trouble, perhaps after the class.

© 2009, Trustees of Boston University. All rights reserved. Center for Psychiatric Rehabilitation.

- **Modifying the content involves eliminating, adding, or changing the activities or pace of the group.** Modifying the content can involve:

    — Eliminating, improving, or adding elaborations, examples, and practice opportunities; or

    — Decreasing or increasing the time spent on a learning activity.

    Modifying the content can be done verbally "on the spot" during the lesson or in writing for a future session of the lesson.

> **Example of Modifying the Content**
>
> **Skill Lesson:** Communicating Anger
>
> **Original Benefit Statement:**
> Communicating Anger lets other people know when you are mad.
>
> Teacher: "So, Barb, can you think of a benefit for being able to communicate your angry feelings?"
>
> Barb: "Well, I guess it would help me feel better."
>
> Teacher: "You would feel relieved if you could say something to people when you're angry."
>
> Barb: "Yeah, and I guess I wouldn't feel like such a fake."
>
> Teacher: "You would feel more genuine if you could tell someone when you are mad at them."
>
> Barb: "Yeah, that's right."
>
> Teacher: "Well, it looks like we have another benefit statement to add to the one I thought of. How does this sound?"
>
> **Tailored Benefit Statement:**
> Communicating Anger allows you to be honest with others about your angry feelings.
>
> Cohen, M., Danley, K., & Nemec, P. (1985, 2007). *Training technology: Direct skills teaching.* Boston: Boston University, Center for Psychiatric Rehabilitation.

- **Modifying the content and/or pace may be done before, during, or after a group.**

    — *Before* the group, modifications may be based on your knowledge of the group members.

    Before your next group activity, what are some examples of content you would modify?

    _____

    _____

    _____

    _____

    _____

    — *During* the group, modifications may be made in the moment.

    What are some examples of instances where you have modified the content and/or the pace during a group activity?

    _____

    _____

    _____

    _____

    _____

    — *After* the group, modifications may be made as a result of the group evaluations and changed for future groups or classes.

    Thinking about your most recent group activity, what are some examples of how you would modify the content for the future?

    _____

    _____

    _____

    _____

    _____

© 2009, Trustees of Boston University. All rights reserved. Center for Psychiatric Rehabilitation.

At times, teachers may feel overly responsible for covering all the content of the class. They may feel they are failing the student if they do not teach the full curriculum.

While it is important to keep to the schedule of the class, it also is natural to fall behind at times. It is better to end the class on time, rather than to go over the allotted class time. Homework can help students to stay current with the curriculum. Begin the next class with the new topic planned in the curriculum.

2.8 Summarizing the Group Activity

Summarizing the Group Activity means the leader goes over the main points discussed during the group activity. A summary is a good review for what content the leader covered and what the participants learned. A summary ties the information together so that people can leave the group feeling finished with the topic for that day.

- **Briefly summarize the purpose of the activity and what had occurred.** For example, *"Today we spent our time learning about how others are recovering from mental illness. We watched a video and then talked about what we'd seen and heard."*

- **Devote a few minutes at the end of each session to ask participants to state what they had learned and/or how they had benefitted from the group activity.** Ask the participants if and how the session had helped them accomplish the outcome that the activity is intended to address. Ask each person to record what he/she has learned or how he/she has benefitted in a notebook.

- **Give directions to the participants about what you want them to do before the next session,** if applicable. For example, *"Think of three questions you would like answered about the process of psychiatric rehabilitation."*

    Briefly introduce the topic of the next session, such as, *"On Thursday we'll begin working on developing a list of things each of you might do to help with your own recovery process."*

Based on your next group activity, outline what you might say in a summary.

_____

_____

_____

_____

_____

_____

_____

This concludes the chapter on Conducting the Group Activity. On the next two pages is a checklist for assessing your delivery skills.

CHECKLIST: Conducting the Group Activity

Name of Group Leader: _____

Name of Group Activity: _____ Date _____

Reviewed the Group Structure and Roles ☐ Yes ☐ No ☐ Partial

Comments _____
_____
_____
_____

Reviewed the Group Objectives ☐ Yes ☐ No ☐ Partial

Comments _____
_____
_____
_____

Oriented to the Activity ☐ Yes ☐ No ☐ Partial

Comments _____
_____
_____
_____

Gave Directions ☐ Yes ☐ No ☐ Partial

Comments _____
_____
_____
_____

© 2009, Trustees of Boston University. All rights reserved. Center for Psychiatric Rehabilitation.

Encouraging Participation

Presented the Activity Content	☐ Yes	☐ No	☐ Partial

Comments _____

_____

_____

_____

_____

Presented to Individuals within a Group	☐ Yes	☐ No	☐ Partial

Comments _____

_____

_____

_____

_____

Modified the Content and/or Pace	☐ Yes	☐ No	☐ Partial

Comments _____

_____

_____

_____

_____

Summarized the Group Activity	☐ Yes	☐ No	☐ Partial

Comments _____

_____

_____

_____

_____

Chapter 3: Encouraging Participation

3.1	Facilitating Introductions
3.2	Attending to the Participants
3.3	Engaging the Participants
3.4	Responding to the Participants
3.5	Responding to Implicit Communication
3.6	Acknowledging Contributions
3.7	Dealing with Challenging Behaviors
3.8	Promoting Problem-Solving
3.9	Promoting Self-Understanding
3.10	Critiquing Participation and Progress
Checklist:	Encouraging Participation

Chapter 3: Encouraging Participation

Encouraging participation is done *during* the group activity. Encouraging participation means inviting full involvement in the group activities. Encouraging participation may help some individuals overcome reluctance and resistance to take part in a group or class. Encouraging participation involves a series of skills:

3.1   Facilitating Introductions

3.2   Attending to the Participants

3.3   Engaging the Participants

3.4   Responding to the Participants

3.5   Responding to Implicit Communication

3.6   Acknowledging Contributions

3.7   Dealing with Challenging Behaviors

3.8   Promoting Problem-Solving

3.9   Promoting Self-Understanding

3.10   Critiquing Participation and Progress

Each one of the encouraging participation skills will be discussed with explanations and suggestions along with examples and practices throughout this chapter.

3.1 Facilitating Introductions

Facilitating Introductions means you bring together people who do not know each other. Facilitating introductions allows the acquaintances to be able to identify each other. When beginning a new group or class, often people do not know each other, and some people may feel awkward or shy. As the group leader, facilitating introductions may help to break the ice for some participants. It usually is helpful to facilitate introductions as soon as possible before the group or class starts, such as when people are just entering the room and finding seats. When facilitating introductions, be sure to:

- **Identify individuals who may not know each other.** You may ask: *"Greg, do you know Joan?"* State each person's name and any connections they may have with each other. For example: *"Greg, Joan worked at the same department store as you did a few years ago. You may know some people in common."* Suggesting a connection may help people to start talking with each other.

As you think about your next group and its members, who in the group might not know each other? What connections might they have in common?

Names of Group Members   *Connections with Other Group Members*

_____   _____

_____   _____

_____   _____

_____   _____

_____   _____

_____   _____

_____   _____

_____   _____

- **Facilitate group introductions by going around the room and asking people to introduce themselves.** Ask participants to be brief and structured in their introductions. Often it helps to role-model an example of what you'd like said by introducing yourself first. For example: *"My name is Sara, and I'm one of the co-leaders for this class, which I have taught two times before."*

    Write down what you would say to introduce yourself and to briefly explain your work experience at the first session of your next group.

    _____

    _____

    _____

    _____

    _____

    _____

    _____

    _____

© 2009, Trustees of Boston University. All rights reserved. Center for Psychiatric Rehabilitation.

There are many ways you can structure the introductions. A couple of suggestions are as follows:

— Ask group members to state their names, where they are from, and why are they taking this class.

— Ask group members to list three things about themselves that they would like others to know.

What is a group introduction exercise that you might like to use?

3.2 Attending to the Participants

Attending to the Participants means to physically pay attention to each participant. Attending engages each group member in a connection with you as the group leader. Attending to the participants involves a couple of behaviors:

- **Make eye contact with each participant.** Sweep the group with your eyes when speaking to the entire group. Make direct eye contact when speaking to an individual. In order to establish and maintain eye contact with individuals, it may be necessary to sit, rather than to stand so that you are on the same eye level with them.

- **Position your body to listen to the participants.** In order to communicate undivided attention to the group members to hear what they say and to see and understand nonverbal behavior, it is important to position your body physically as much as possible throughout the activity. Stand in a location that provides a clear line of sight with as many people as possible. Square your shoulders towards a person when interacting with him or her. Maintain an open posture by standing straight with your arms open rather than folded. Lean slightly towards an individual as he or she speaks, especially if the content is emotionally charged, or if you are having difficulty hearing the person or understanding what he or she is saying. Maintain an overall relaxed posture.

3.3 Engaging the Participants

Engaging the Participants means connecting with each of the group members. Engaging involves relating the participant's experiences with the group activity, which provides a point of connection and a personal reason for taking part in the group activity. Attempt to involve each person to actively participate in each group session. Engaging the participants involves several techniques:

- **Greet each participant by name at the beginning of the activity.** Most people like to feel acknowledged and to feel that their presence is appreciated.

- **Ask open-ended questions to facilitate exploration.** Ask questions that you think everyone can answer. For example: *"What is at least one thing that you like about being here?"* vs. *"Is there at least one thing that you like about being here?"* Or: *"What is one thing that you like or dislike about this place?"* vs. *"What is it like for you being here?"*

    — Direct questions usually are answered with "yes," "no," or one-word answers. They are meant to generate specific information from the individual. Example of a direct question: *"What is your supervisor's name?"*

    What are some examples of direct questions that you might need to know about when starting your group or class?

    _____
    _____
    _____
    _____
    _____
    _____
    _____
    _____

    — Open-ended questions usually are not answered with "yes," "no," or one-word answers. They are meant to elicit exploration or free sharing of the individual's thoughts.

    Example of an open-ended question: *"What do you like about your supervisor?"*

© 2009, Trustees of Boston University. All rights reserved. Center for Psychiatric Rehabilitation.

What are some examples of open-ended questions that you might ask to generate a discussion in your next group or activity?

- **Ask frequently for group members' input, opinions, perceptions, and experiences.** This allows participants to have a voice in shaping the class discussions.

- **Review the participants' experiences with the activity content.** For example: *"What does the term 'values' mean to you? Have you ever participated in any values clarification activities?"*

    Asking questions about knowledge of the content of the activity allows the leader to gain initial understanding before teaching or leading a group. It engages the participants early on.

    What are some examples of questions you might ask to review the activity content in your next group or activity?

- **Connect the participants' experiences to the activity content.** Respond to questions or comments by group members. Make connections between what they say to the content of the lesson. For example: *"José, you said that it's important to make eye contact when interviewing for a job, and that is one of the steps of the skill."*

    Based on your knowledge of your group participants, what are some connections with the activity content they have experienced?

Names of Group Members	*Connections with Activity Content*

- **Make comments that address the group as a whole,** such as: *"This issue seems to raise a lot of feelings for many of you."* This type of universal statement helps to connect participants so that they may not feel so alone with their feelings.

- **Use of humor can be very effective and engaging.** As the group leader, you don't need to be a stand-up comic, but occasional jokes that relate to the activity content may be fun and may lighten the atmosphere during a class.

- **Call upon silent group members for specific information or personal experiences to engage them and to raise them to a higher level of participation.** This is a delicate skill to perform. You need to think about the quiet individuals and assess whether they are quiet because of shyness or because they may not know what to contribute. Be sure to ask questions that you are fairly certain that they can answer, otherwise, they may feel embarrassed and even less likely to contribute in the future.

© 2009, Trustees of Boston University. All rights reserved. Center for Psychiatric Rehabilitation.

Who are some quiet group members in your group or class? What questions might you ask them?

Names of Quiet Group Members	Questions to Ask
_____	_____
_____	_____
_____	_____
_____	_____
_____	_____
_____	_____
_____	_____
_____	_____

- **Paraphrase questions asked by participants.** This can be very helpful, especially in large groups so that people can hear the question. This also helps to clarify your understanding of the question. If your paraphrase is incorrect, then the person asking the question is likely to rephrase their question for you.

3.4 Responding to the Participants

Responding to the Participants means replying to comments that group members have made in class. Responding demonstrates your understanding of what they have said. Responding or demonstrating understanding is describing what another person is saying and/or feeling. Demonstrating understanding is capturing in words what the other person's thoughts, feelings, and/or reasons for the feelings. Demonstrating understanding acknowledges the importance of what the other person has said. Demonstrating understanding can be used to stimulate the person to talk further. Respond to the participants if you want to encourage more exploration, to clarify what the person is saying, or to establish or maintain a personal connection with the individual.

Respect the participants' thoughts, feelings, and experiences. Respect will support individuals when they feel most vulnerable. Validation is an important role of the leaders. Feelings and experiences associated with trust, safety, loneliness, family issues, medication, shame, and work are common issues that will be addressed by many group members. Issues raised by the group members provide opportunities for validation, as well as providing knowledge, skills, and resources for support.

According to Robert Carkhuff (2000), there are several types of responses you may make:

- **Responding to Content involves accurately summarizing what the person has shared about his/her situation.**
    - Example: *"You're saying that your supervisor treats you with respect."*
    - Format: *You're saying that* _____.

    Practice statement: *"My class just started last week, and there are three more classes to go. I'm not sure if there is enough time to cover everything I want to learn."*

    Response to Content:

    _____
    _____
    _____
    _____
    _____
    _____

- **Responding to Feelings involves accurately reflecting a feeling word that is interchangeable with the person's experience of the situation.**
    - Example: *"You feel appreciated."*
    - Format: *You feel* _____.

    Practice statement: *"I just discovered that I am missing $20 from my wallet."*

    Response to Feelings:

    _____
    _____
    _____
    _____
    _____
    _____

- **Responding to Feeling and Meaning involves accurately reflecting both the feeling and the content expressed by the person in a manner which is interchangeable with their statement.**

    — Example: *"You feel trusted because he encourages you to work independently."*
    "You feel irritated because he canceled your supervision appointment."

    — Format: *You feel _____ because _____.*

    Practice statement: *"My roommate seems to be interested in my boyfriend. She keeps flirting with him when he comes over to see me. Sometimes she doesn't relay messages that he has called me."*

    Response to Feeling & Meaning:

    _____
    _____
    _____
    _____
    _____

Participation usually is increased when the group leader makes statements in response to individuals that demonstrate an accurate understanding of his/her thoughts, feelings, beliefs, and experiences. The educational focus of the teaching can be emphasized further by not interpreting students' comments. Avoid interpretation in this educational setting. Interpretation is a therapeutic intervention and does not have a role in education.

Some additional tips for Responding:

- **Respond directly to the content, feelings, and meanings of what the individual says.** Leaders should remain in the present.

- **Create a balance between facilitating the activity vs. listening and responding.** A teacher's active presence and involvement is important to students. Communication between the teacher and the students can be as valuable as the content you are teaching. While the primary goal of teaching is conveying information, listening is also an important skill. Create a balance between what you have to say and listening and responding to what the students have to say.

- **Be as accurate as possible in identifying a group member's strong feelings.** Difficulties can emerge in identifying, labeling, and managing strong feelings during the class. Individuals may have learned to be fearful about intense feelings because of the strong feelings of others in their own lives may have been difficult to handle, and they also may fear the eruption of their own feelings. Teachers also may be wary of managing strong feelings. We can learn to respond safely to our own fears and to the feelings of others. Learning how to feel safe with feelings as they arise and resolve themselves requires time and a safe environment, which is provided by the classroom setting.

- **Avoid trying to solve feelings raised in the class, instead respond to the feelings.** Listen to them and validate them, for example:
    - *"I hear how angry you are."*
    - *"I hear how distressful this has been."*

- **Help participants to articulate their feelings that can validate these emotions and can limit overwhelming them.** Strong feelings can increase very quickly, particularly when the focus shifts to the content of the communication rather than the feelings.

- **Ask if someone else in the class has had a similar experience.** Usually, it is easier to bear a strong feeling if individuals know that other people have experienced it, too.

- **Help group members to express feelings in a safe environment to help them to manage their strong emotions and to feel safe with them.** Learning to feel safe with strong emotions may take some time if participants have learned to protect themselves from their feelings. People can learn that feelings can come, can grow, and if acknowledged and validated, can diminish. There is a natural cycle to our feelings. This knowledge of the cycle of feelings can be an important learning for some people. Individuals, who may have learned not to express their feelings, may feel that they will be overwhelmed by them, or that others may perceive their emotions as symptoms of an illness. Acknowledging, respecting, validating, and experiencing feelings in the class can help people to rediscover the "feeling side" of themselves.

- **Help individuals to express their feelings more directly by putting them into words rather than actions.** Participants may "act" on their feelings in subtle ways, such as coming late, complaining, projecting their feelings onto others, or becoming withdrawn. Identifying the source of feelings may be helpful for people. Ask questions, such as:
    - *"What is making you angry now?"*
    - *"What is making you sad now?"*
    - *"What is making you fearful now?"*

    When anticipating that someone may have sensitive feelings about an issue or topic, you may want to talk with them individually outside of the group, instead of with others during the class.

- **Do not explore the past source of feelings, simply identify it and the feelings it evokes. Focus on the present.** Stay in the here and now. You might ask,
    - *"Is there something happening now that is making you feel this way?"*
    - *"How are you being affected right now?"*
    - *"What would be helpful in dealing with this situation?"*
    - *"What information or support do you need?"*
    - *"Who else in the class has dealt with this situation successfully?"*

© 2009, Trustees of Boston University. All rights reserved. Center for Psychiatric Rehabilitation.

3.5 Responding to Implicit Communication

Responding to Implicit Communication means responding to communication that is indirect and has hidden or unconscious meanings. Students often use metaphors unconsciously or implicit communication to deal with feelings stimulated within the class. For example, comments on an authority figure might refer to feelings about the leader; negative self-references might suggest that the individual believes others hold similar negative feelings toward him or her; or descriptions of conflicts outside the class might suggest a student is struggling with feelings of disconnection from class members. This is particularly relevant if the implicit communications are repeated frequently. Thus, important underlying issues, such as safety, blame, trust, or rejection might emerge as implicit communications.

- **Assume that issues students are describing are related to experiences they are having in the present class.** This does not negate descriptions of the students' explicit experiences, nor does it mean interpreting what students are saying. It brings the implicit reality of their internal habits of experiencing their world into the present where they can be explored.

- **Ask participants whether what they are saying or feeling connects to what they are currently experiencing in the class.** Students' use of implicit communication suggests that some sense of risk is perceived consciously or unconsciously. Respect this potential risk.

- **Respond in terms of the present context,** which can feel safer for the person and may redirect the participants' natural tendencies to "talk about" their experiences and to live them in the present.

3.6 Acknowledging Contributions

Acknowledging Contributions means recognizing individual and group efforts made during the group or class. Acknowledging contributions demonstrates respect for the participants' attempts to improve the group activity for themselves and for others. Crediting contributions can help reduce anxiety about participating in a group. Anxiety may be from old experiences with learning in school. Some ways to acknowledge contributions include:

- **Paraphrase participants' statements by restating a comment made.** Paraphrasing shows that you understood the point that they have made. Or, if you have misunderstood, then the individual has the chance to clarify his or her remark.

- **Credit the participants' input by stating who said what point.**

- **Connect the participants' input to the content.** It is critical to make the connection between what a group member has said and how it relates to the points being made in class. If there is remark made that does not relate, then the leader has a chance to reshape the comment to make it more relevant. Usually, there is some part of a comment that does relate to the content. For example: *"Mike, you said that responding to feelings is like responding to flowers. So you're saying that when you respond to the feelings of someone, you help them grow, kind of like when you're watering flowers."*

- **Praise the participant for the contribution.** Offer praise and encouragement frequently. Most people appreciate the acknowledgement publically, or at least, privately.

What are some examples of how you have acknowledged contributions in your groups?

___

___

___

___

___

___

___

___

___

3.7 Dealing with Challenging Behaviors

Dealing with Challenging Behaviors means managing non-contributive behaviors. Dealing with challenging behaviors maximizes conditions which support learning for others in the group activity. There are a number of behaviors that are challenging at times to teachers and other students. These include when someone monopolizes the conversation, when someone is often late, and when there is an ongoing conflict between two students. Dealing with challenging behaviors involves several techniques:

- **Orient people to the process of the group.** Review the behavioral expectations for the group at the beginning of the group or class when reviewing the class structure and roles. As discussed in chapter 2, sometimes these behavioral expectations need to be repeated periodically.

- **Evaluate the merit of an individual's contribution and assess the severity of the distraction.** If comments are not relevant to the particular topic, this probably is a distraction.

- **Balance the respect of an individual with the comfort of others in a group.** Balance between tolerance of the behavior and watchfulness that the behavior doesn't worsen or that it offends others in the group.

- **Choose the level of responsiveness to each challenging behavior.** The LEAST approach (adapted from Carkhuff, 1981) offers a structure for how to respond to individuals that can be very effective. LEAST stands for:

    — **L**eave it alone. Ignore the behavior and often it will cease.

    — **E**ye contact. Make eye contact with the individual, indicating that you are hearing what is being said, but that you are not going to address it verbally at that moment.

    — **A**ttend to it directly. Share your observations within the group. A simple statement might be made, such as: *"Bill, you've answered my question and made some interesting points. How about if we give someone else a chance to respond?"*

    — **S**trategize. Sometimes you will need to take a break and talk to the person individually outside of the group. Set up a meeting with the person to share your observations and describe his or her behavior in the group. You might need to ask the person, *"What can you do differently to meet the class expectations?"*

    — **T**erminate the role (at least temporarily). Sometimes people experience difficulties in groups, especially if they are having a hard time with symptoms. Sometimes it helps to allow a person to select out of a group at that time. They sometimes may feel relieved to terminate their participation in the group. In order for the person to not feel rejected from the group, it is important to be clear to invite the person to return to the group or class when feeling more ready to participate according to the group's expectations.

    Recount an example where you might have used the LEAST approach in one of your groups or classes.

    _____
    _____
    _____
    _____
    _____
    _____
    _____
    _____

- **Develop and implement a behavior management plan.** A behavior management plan is an agreement between the group leader and the participant that outlines what he or she is supposed to do in order to remain in the group or class. This plan may include similar behaviors that were listed in the group's expectations, but it is more personalized to the individual. This plan may include rewards for behaviors performed well and consequences for inappropriate behaviors.

Below are some examples of some challenging behaviors and group leader responses:

— Sometimes individuals seem to talk too much. They may not leave space for others to talk. One intervention might be to have people agree early in the first class to limit comments to a couple of minutes because time is limited and everyone is encouraged to participate. Periodic reminders of this agreement can be a gentle way of limiting conversation. In the moment, you also might ask someone who is taking too much time to summarize in one or two sentences what he or she is trying to say. Simplifying comments makes them easier for others to understand.

— Some students are habitually late for class. However, it is important to always start the class on time. The initial agreement for the class reinforces this expectation. Remember, that the agreements made at the start of the classes are primarily a commitment people make to themselves. It is assumed that coming to the class was their decision, and they made the decision to improve their lives. When someone is frequently late, remind him or her privately of the agreement they made when the class started. Also, remind the person that they are important, and that the class is not the same when they are not present from the start. Help the person think through steps to overcome practical obstacles to being on time. This is an opportunity to help the student feel successful. However, sometimes people are legitimately late (e.g., transportation problems) and should not be "shamed" about this.

— Personal conflicts are common in classes and groups. People have natural needs to feel safe, recognized, valued, and to be special. They also want to be a contributing member of the class. Yet, at times, students also may be vulnerable to competitiveness with one another. This can lead to strong feelings between students. Situations of personal conflict need to be identified as soon as possible. Once identified, the people involved need to be made aware of the conflict and its impact on their own learning and on the class. Talking to those students involved outside of the class can be helpful. Keep in mind that conflicts are not problems, but solutions that students arrive at to take care of themselves. You might ask, *"How could your behavior be different in this class? How can you get what you want rather than becoming involved in conflict?"*

Helping people to find new ways to get what they want sometimes can resolve the conflict sufficiently to enable them to benefit from the class experience. At times, students need to be encouraged to take a break from attending the class and to work on their personal issues before returning.

What are some examples of challenging behaviors that have occurred in your groups or classes, and how have you dealt with them?

_____
_____
_____
_____
_____
_____
_____
_____
_____

3.8 Promoting Problem-Solving

Promoting Problem-Solving is helping individuals to find solutions to their problems. Promoting problem-solving supports people to overcome barriers to their problems. Promoting problem-solving teaches people to become more self-reliant when dealing with difficult situations. There are many ways to promote problem-solving:

- **Ask participants to share how they have dealt with problems, when issues come up in class.** Ask them to be specific. Other group members can be valuable resources for one another because they already have dealt with a great many problematic situations. Asking for suggestions for the student can be challenging. The teacher and student want suggestions that have come from personal experience or the experience of people they know. Advice that does not come from personal experience can overwhelm the student and make him or her feel stupid and helpless. Giving advice also can be a way of distancing ourselves from others. It suggests not wanting to listen to the feelings and frustrations students are feeling as they describe their struggles. Giving advice may take care of us, but not the person who is struggling.

- **Acknowledge the person's success and ongoing efforts to be active participants in their lives.** Validation builds self-esteem and confidence. Other students may have had similar situations and could share how they have handled them successfully.

- **Provide students with information and resources that can be helpful when group members present a crisis situation they are currently experiencing.** Refer people to resources in the community related to their issue.

- **Meet with the person outside of class and provide consultation and support.** However, the goal of the class is not to solve students' issues, but rather, to educate them so that they have the knowledge, skills, resources, and support to resolve crisis situations.

Another way of saying this is that one purpose of the class is to move students from a reactive mode to a responsive one. A reactive mode may include panic, anxiety, confusion, lack of confidence, lack of knowledge of resources, hopelessness, and a lack of clarity concerning practical steps for resolving crises. A responsive mode includes the opposite of a reactive mode—it means that students are confident and ready to actively explore ways to solve issues that arise. Providing students with knowledge, skills, resources, and supports can begin to move them toward a more ongoing responsive mode.

- **When confronted with a repetitive problematic situation, ask the group members what is preventing them from building a life for themselves.** Ask: *"Why are you getting stuck in this issue?"* The question is not how to resolve every issue or to become "normal." The question is how to become oneself; and to build a life that respects oneself, with one's own limitations, assets, skills, and abilities.

- **Explore the barriers to building a self-affirming life.** Ask students to be specific. Understanding the perceived barriers can be important because it validates the students' experiences. Be brief in searching for and acknowledging barriers.

- **Focus on setting personal goals related to problematic situations and developing practical steps, skills, and supports to achieve the individual's goal.** Setting goals moves people from a helpless position to a helpful position in life.

- **Support participants in identifying what would be helpful with respect to knowledge, skills, or support to achieve their goals.** Encourage students to be specific. Other students, who have dealt successfully with similar problematic situations, can be helpful.

- **Teaching knowledge or skills related to specific issues raised in class can be helpful to students.** These may include relationship skills, stress management skills, symptom management skills, and emotional skills. If the teaching is to have an impact, adding the teaching of a specific knowledge or skill content, as a supplement to what is already being covered in the class, should be connected to what is acknowledged explicitly by students as needed.

What are some examples of problem-solving techniques you have used in your groups or classes?

_____

_____

_____

_____

_____

_____

_____

© 2009, Trustees of Boston University. All rights reserved. Center for Psychiatric Rehabilitation.

3.9 Promoting Self-Understanding

Promoting Self-Understanding means to be aware of oneself, specifically personality traits and behaviors. Even when people have self-understanding and insight, changing their sense of self often is perceived as "risky." As the sense of self is reorganized, new understanding can bring fears of disorganization, shame, or loss of control.

- **Let students know that change confronts the way we are currently, and at times can be stressful.** This is especially true when we are in the midst of it, such as when we are giving up old perceptions or behaviors and have not yet adopted new ones. This can be a confusing and painful transition. Understanding the change process and getting support during it are helpful strategies for anyone committed to change.

- **Mirroring or seeing ourselves in others is an important source of learning.** Helping participants to acknowledge how others have helped them can be useful. For example, *"It sounds like how Bill handled that situation he was talking about last week was helpful to you."*

- **Help people to remain in the present by responding to past concerns,** such as:
  — *"How would you handle this now?"*
  — *"How would this be different for you now?"*
  — *"What feelings does this bring up for you now?"*

  Understanding and insight usually come from the present situations rather than from the past.

- **Respect the slow process of change.** Change takes time and it tends to occur in stages. Learning is a gradual unfolding of our awareness and competency. Given a supportive and informative environment, change is more likely to happen. With patience, time, effort, personalizing the learning, and the opportunity for individuals to build self-confidence, change has a good chance.

- **Respect the ambiguity of change.** Sometimes it may look as if nothing is happening or that a person is losing ground. However, feeling threatened, confused, and stuck is a natural part of the learning process. When people are distressed, they tend to revert to more familiar thinking and behaving. This rarely lasts. It is just a phase in the process. Learn to tolerate not knowing and to trust in the unfolding of the process.

- **Respect the person's need to be confused, and then to integrate and consolidate new learning.**

- **Respect the feeling of caution.** Family members and individuals with mental illnesses may have been bruised and battered in their relationships. Trusting helpers may be limited by prior frustrations and disappointments. Some individuals may enter new relationships cautiously and let others into their world slowly.

- **Respect the increased vulnerability that comes with any change process.** Change shifts the sense of self. People can become uncomfortable as they let go of old ways of being and adopt new ones that are unfamiliar. Let them know this is a natural process for everyone. Change is unsettling. It shakes us up on the way to settling us down.

- **Respectful feedback is an important way to connect with individuals who are naturally cautious and vulnerable.** It is important that feedback focus on the students' progress toward their goals. Consistent and generous positive feedback on students' progress is very important. People want to know that they are gradually achieving their goals, each at his or her own pace. The expectation that students can achieve their goals is imbedded in this feedback process. More information about feedback in discussed in the next section, Critiquing Participation and Progress.

- **Help participants to see what their barriers are, if their progress is slow or stuck.** Also, help them to appreciate their often slow and ongoing struggle to reach their goal. This is a normal part of any learning process. Change, even when we want it, is often a struggle and can move along at a very slow pace.

3.10 Critiquing Participation and Progress

Critiquing Participation and Progress is leading the individual through an assessment of his or her performance in an activity and future learning needs. Critiquing participation and progress develops a shared understanding of the individual's present performance and future learning needs. Giving feedback is an interactive process. Be sure to get the other person's perspective first before giving yours. Self-critiquing is a form of discrimination of knowledge of the skill or activity. Critiquing participation and progress involves the following techniques:

- **Describe the individual's performance in the activity by stating what you actually saw the person do or heard the person say.** Describing performance in the activity assures a mutual understanding of the individual's performance. To describe performance:

    — Observe the performance of the participant

    — Reflect on the performance criteria

    — Explain to the participant what you have observed

    — Use clear language that illustrates what you have observed

    Example: *"Carla, you did a very nice job presenting your lecture on Taking Notes in a class. You explained clearly how to listen carefully to the instructor, to identify the key points, and to record the points in a logical way. You gave lots of good tips about how to make your notes clear."*

    What are some performance criteria for a skill you are teaching in your group or class?

    _____

    _____

    _____

    _____

© 2009, Trustees of Boston University. All rights reserved. Center for Psychiatric Rehabilitation.

- **Identify key strengths and areas for improvement by naming the essential behaviors that were and were not performed accurately.** Identifying key strengths and areas for improvement recognizes achievement and identifies future learning needs. Focus on building new skills and competencies. Identify students' existing interests and abilities in helping them select areas to initiate action. Do not focus on how people have not been succeeding. Refocus the person's efforts on coming up with new solutions. Remind people that it is natural to keep doing what is familiar even when it isn't working. The way out of our ingrained habits is to try something else, with support.

Fortunately, in any class there usually are students who have succeeded in areas where others have not. These students are important resources for the class. If someone feels stuck with a particular issue, ask the class members if they have had a similar experience and what solutions have worked for them. Avoid directly solving someone's issue. You and the class members are there to provide information and support, not answers.

Identifying key strengths and areas for improvement involves several techniques:

— Observe performance of the participants

— Assess the participant's performance against criteria

— Name at least one important strength

— Name no more than one or two important area(s) for improvement

Example: *"Carla, your biggest strength was that you were very good in your explanations in your lecture on Taking Notes. You followed your outline well, and you explained the steps very clearly and logically. The one area for improvement is that for me, since I'm a visual learner, I would have liked to have seen more examples."*

List some strengths and one area for improvement for someone you are teaching in your group or class.

- **Define additional learning activities by outlining sources and actions to help the students increase knowledge and improve skill performance.** Defining additional learning activities creates opportunities for developing additional strengths. Defining additional learning activities involves meeting with the participant to:

  — Reflect on the key area or two that needs improvement

  — Structure practice exercises that will strengthen that area

  — Review progress with the area that needs improvement

  Example: *"Carla, as I mentioned, I would have liked to have seen more examples in your lecture on Taking Notes. My suggestion for improvement for you is that I would like to see on paper what a good page of notes looks like."*

  What are some additional learning activities you might suggest to someone who needs to improve skill performance?

  _____

  _____

  _____

  _____

  _____

  _____

  _____

  _____

  _____

  Because of the sensitive nature of receiving feedback for most people, it is critical for you to demonstrate understanding of the other person's reaction to your feedback while critiquing performance and participation. This is a time to be extra empathetic and supportive.

The section on Encouraging Participation is completed. The checklist for assessing your skills in Encouraging Participation is included on the next two pages.

© 2009, Trustees of Boston University. All rights reserved. Center for Psychiatric Rehabilitation.

CHECKLIST: Encouraging Participation

Name of Group Leader: _____

Name of Group Activity: _____ Date _____

Facilitated Introductions	☐ Yes	☐ No	☐ Partial

Comments _____
_____
_____

Attended to the Participants	☐ Yes	☐ No	☐ Partial

Comments _____
_____
_____

Engaged the Participants	☐ Yes	☐ No	☐ Partial

Comments _____
_____
_____

Responded to the Participants	☐ Yes	☐ No	☐ Partial

Comments _____
_____
_____

Responded to Implicit Communication	☐ Yes	☐ No	☐ Partial

Comments _____
_____
_____

© 2009, Trustees of Boston University. All rights reserved. Center for Psychiatric Rehabilitation.

Acknowledged Contributions   ☐ Yes   ☐ No   ☐ Partial

Comments _____

_____

_____

Dealt with Challenging Behaviors   ☐ Yes   ☐ No   ☐ Partial

Comments _____

_____

_____

Promoted Problem-Solving   ☐ Yes   ☐ No   ☐ Partial

Comments _____

_____

_____

Promoted Self-Understanding   ☐ Yes   ☐ No   ☐ Partial

Comments _____

_____

_____

Critiqued Participation and Progress   ☐ Yes   ☐ No   ☐ Partial

Comments _____

_____

_____

© 2009, Trustees of Boston University. All rights reserved. Center for Psychiatric Rehabilitation.

Encouraging Participation | GROUP PROCESS GUIDELINES FOR LEADING GROUPS AND CLASSES

Chapter 4: Promoting Peer Leadership

4.1	Encouraging Peer-to-Peer Interactions
4.2	Self-Disclosing
4.3	Incorporating Experiences into Content
4.4	Collaborating with Peers
4.5	Supporting Peer Leaders
Checklist:	Promoting Peer Leadership

Chapter 4: Promoting Peer Leadership

Promoting peer leadership is encouraging peers to assist in facilitating a group or to fully lead a group. There are natural leaders within any group of people. Sometimes leaders naturally emerge, and sometimes leaders need to be developed. Promoting peer leadership involves a series of skills:

4.1   Encouraging Peer-to-Peer Interactions

4.2   Self-Disclosing

4.3   Incorporating Experiences into Content

4.4   Collaborating with Peers

4.5   Supporting Peer Leaders

Each of the skills in promoting peer leadership will be discussed with explanations and suggestions, and examples and practices will be sprinkled throughout this chapter.

4.1 Encouraging Peer-to-Peer Interactions

Encouraging Peer-to-Peer Interactions involves actively requesting participants to talk among themselves about the activity content, what they are learning, and the impact of what they are learning. Helping students to connect with each other is an important role of the teacher. Students enter the class as individuals. One of the leader's goals is that they will leave feeling more connected to one another. Many techniques may be used to encourage peer-to-peer interactions.

- **Use name tags as a way of identifying people during the first group meeting.** The sooner students engage with each other in the class, the more likely they will continue to engage in the class and participate actively.

- **Encourage students to say their name and something brief about their experience at the beginning of the first class meeting.** This exercise helps students begin to talk. As discussed in chapter 3, section 3.1 Facilitating Introductions, you might want to role model what to say.

- **Involve participants in brief small group exercises.** Students connect by sharing similar experiences, feelings, and activities. Connecting exercises in small groups of two or three people can provide an opportunity for students to get to know one another. For example, you may create a short exercise of asking participants to name one thing that they like about their roommate or their co-worker.

    Identify an initial connecting exercise you might use for your new group.

    _____

    _____

    _____

    _____

© 2009, Trustees of Boston University. All rights reserved. Center for Psychiatric Rehabilitation.

- **Ask students to report on homework during each class to encourage them to talk.** Limit self-disclosure and reporting on homework to two minutes. Sometimes specific questions are helpful, such as, *"What do people think of what we have just read?"* However, do not pressure people who are reticent to participate. Some people learn silently. Others take time to feel comfortable enough to participate.

- **Encourage group members to build relationships with each other.** It is natural and helpful for the students to relate to each other during the class and also to contact one another outside of the class. For example, participants can connect through phone calls between class sessions. Ask permission of the group members to have their names, phone numbers, and e-mail addresses listed so they can contact one another. It can be useful to have students agree to call two other students during the week to see how the class is going for them. This active exercise will help more reserved class members to connect with others. If needed, you might want to suggest a time limit for these phone calls.

- **Attend to any conflicts that are brought to your attention that occur between students outside of the class.** Often what happens outside of the group between participants is grist for the mill because it may affect the learning process within the class. Respond empathetically to the participants and avoid any appearance of "taking sides" in a conflict.

- **Continue connecting activities for the students during each of the classes because learning to connect is a process and not an event.** Brief, ongoing exercises can facilitate the connecting process. For example, *ask participants to think of three things they did for themselves during the past week and three things they could do for themselves during the coming week to stimulate awareness of the need for self-care.* Participants' responses can be shared in small groups and reported on to the larger group. Similar non-threatening exercises provide students with ongoing opportunities for personal connecting in the class.

    Identify a connecting exercise you might use for your ongoing group.

    _____
    _____
    _____
    _____
    _____

- **Ask participants to give helpful input or to give support to other group members.** For example, *ask them to suggest ways that an individual may use a skill, recognize a personal strength, or learn more about what he or she wants in a place to live or work.*

- **Ask participants to present information or to demonstrate a skill to the group.** For example, *explain what different types of mental health services are offered in the community.*

What are some examples of how participants could present information and give demonstrations in your group or class?

_____
_____
_____
_____
_____

4.2 Self-Disclosing

Self-Disclosing is sharing your ideas, experiences, and/or beliefs with another person. Self-disclosing can be used to demonstrate empathy for the other person by sharing similar personal ideas, experiences, and/or beliefs. Self-disclosing is especially helpful with peer leaders because of similar experiences peer leaders may have had with the other group participants. Participants will naturally assume some affinity with a peer leader and with one another group member. Peer leaders often can be seen as role models to other group members. Thus, self-disclosures from a peer leader may be viewed as more impactful.

Self-disclosing involves a couple of steps:

- **Formulate your disclosure by mentally summarizing the idea, experience, or belief to share.** Self-disclosures should be used sparingly, so it is very important to think through what you would say in a self-disclosure.

- **Select the best type of self-disclosure statement to share given the situation and conversation you are having with someone.** There are several types of self-disclosure statements (Cohen, Nemec, Farkas, Forbess, & Cohen, 1988, 2007):

    — **Describing** is used to elaborate on your own ideas or beliefs.

    Example of a Describing statement: *"I think your counselor is probably trying to protect you from the possibility of making a mistake."*

    Formats for Describing statements:
    - *I think/thought (ideas) about (topic).*
    - *In my opinion (opinion).*
    - *I intend to (intention).*
    - *I believe (value) is very important.*
    - *I try to (ethics) whenever possible.*
    - *I believe (assumption) is true.*

    Practice statement: *"I've lived at the group home for two months now, and the rules keep changing."*

© 2009, Trustees of Boston University. All rights reserved. Center for Psychiatric Rehabilitation.

Describing statement:

— **Genuineness** is used to express your own emotional feeling about events of personal significance.

Example of a Genuineness statement: *"I remember when I wanted to try and take an advanced math course. I felt ready, but no one believed me. It was so frustrating."*

Formats for Genuineness statements:

- *I feel (feeling word).*
- *I feel (feeling word) because (event) happened.*
- *I felt (feeling word).*
- *I felt (feeling word) because (event happened).*
- *I (feeling word) about (situation).*
- *I was (feeling word) because I (personal significance).*
- *I did (actions) when they did (actions).*
- *When I did (action), I (experience).*
- *In my experience, I've found (experience).*

Practice statement: *"I don't trust my supervisor at work. She changes her mind constantly, and she also seems to make up things. I don't believe what she says most of the time."*

Genuineness statement:

- **Immediacy** is used when a person wants to share personal reactions to the other person and their relationship.

    Example of an Immediacy statement: *"Jane, I'm confident that if you say you're ready to return to school, then you are ready. In our relationship, you've shown that you know when you are ready to take the next step."*

    Formats for Immediacy statements:

    - *I feel (feeling word) about you.*
    - *I feel (feeling word) about (your action).*
    - *I feel (feeling word) about (aspect of our relationship).*
    - *I feel (feeling word) about (our interaction).*

    Practice statement: *"We've worked together for six months now. I think I've come a long way."*

    Immediacy statement:

    _____
    _____
    _____
    _____
    _____
    _____

- **Disagreeing** is used to contrast differences in two people's perspectives.

    Example of a Disagreeing statement: *"John, you think you are ready to start work right away, but I think you need to take the time to explore whether kitchen work is the best type of job for you now."*

    Formats for Disagreeing statements:

    - *I think (my idea), while you think (your idea).*
    - *On the one hand, you think (your idea), but I think (my idea).*
    - *In my experience (what happened to me), while you experienced (what happened to you).*
    - *You've said you believe (your belief), but I believe (my belief).*
    - *I feel (my experience), while you feel (your experience).*

    Practice statement: *"I think I did really well on that practice exercise for a job interview."*

© 2009, Trustees of Boston University. All rights reserved. Center for Psychiatric Rehabilitation.

Disagreeing statement:

_____

_____

_____

_____

_____

_____

- **Choose whether to share the disclosure based on the relevance of what your disclosure to what is being discussed, the readiness for the other person to hear it, and the probable impact of your statement on the other person.** Will your self-disclosure be helpful or not? Check out with the group participants how they felt about your self-disclosure. You will want to know how it has impacted them. If the impact is negative or seen as a distraction from the participant's own disclosure, you might want to consider not self-disclosing.

Some additional tips for Self-Disclosing:

- **Do not use self-disclosure early on to establish a relationship.** Skillful and competent understanding and empathy are better tools to establish a relationship.

- **Use self-disclosure minimally until you have developed a relationship of trust and safety with the individual.** Self-disclosure is a sharing of intimacy that should not be rushed into by either person. When a person rushes into intimacy, he or she may have a reaction of shame or embarrassment that can create greater anxiety and tension rather than reduce it. We cannot assume that the other person will feel safe and trust us simply because we are in the helping role. Disclosure on the part of the student we are teaching is built on the trust and safety earned by the peer leader through his or her genuine and skillful understanding and empathy.

Self-disclosure requires a well-developed sense of self and good self-esteem. When we know ourselves well, we are less likely to be using the relationship and the self-disclosure for our own benefit and interests. When our self-disclosure comes from our knowledge of ourselves, it is more likely to be helpful. When a relationship has been developed, the peer leader is in a better position to target his or her self-disclosure in a helpful way. When our self-disclosure comes from our knowledge of the other person, it is more likely to be helpful.

- **Refrain from using self-disclosure as a response to self-disclosure. This could be viewed as trying to one-up the other person.** A more helpful response would be to empathize with the experience of the student. When someone is self-disclosing to us, we do not want to change the focus of the conversation to ourselves. The other person could see this as a discount or rejection. Also, when someone is sharing something important with us, we need to listen carefully and to respond with empathy.

- **Keep self-disclosures brief.** Remember, you don't want to take over the group or change the topic of the conversation. Briefly state your self-disclosure, and then connect your self-disclosure with the group member's issue or topic of conversation. Be brief and return to the individual with full attention, understanding, and empathy.

- **Display emotions congruent with what the other person is expressing.** Remember, self-disclosure is an empathic response meant to show the other person that you understand what he or she is experiencing, and is not a cheerleading (positive self-disclosure) or overdramatic (negative self-disclosure) response.

- **Use of positive self-disclosure content can model possibilities and may help to inspire and motivate the group members to go beyond their current level of expectations.** Use of negative self-disclosure content can "normalize" feelings or experiences that seem overwhelming or out of control to people. It can be helpful to know that other people struggle or are imperfect, even the group leader. Also, if you are disclosing ambivalence, disclose both sides of the issue.

- **Changing the subject is a way of avoiding our anxiety and fear of being with the person in their pain.** This is how the individual might experience it. Changing the subject happens often in conversations, and we end up feeling derailed. We know what it is like when someone does not seem to be listening to us or does not seem to be interested in us. We know how we feel when someone does that with us, so you will want to avoid doing that to another person.

- **If a participant asks a direct question about you as the peer leader, it usually is more useful to first ask the person why he or she is curious about you.** In our experience, when you respond this way, the individual often gets back into his or her own story and forgets the question. If the participant brings it up again, then you can decide whether or not to self-disclose.

Describe a situation when you used self-disclosure in a group or class where it worked well.

_____
_____
_____
_____
_____

Describe a situation when you used self-disclosure in a group or class where it did not work very well.

_____
_____
_____
_____
_____

© 2009, Trustees of Boston University. All rights reserved. Center for Psychiatric Rehabilitation.

If you could have had the chance to erase what you said, what would you have done differently?

_____
_____
_____
_____
_____

4.3 Incorporating Experiences into Content

Incorporating Experiences into Content means you intertwine personal accounts into the subject matter of the group or class. Incorporating experiences into the content is extremely important because it shows the participants that your experience and/or their experience is relevant to the discussion content. In a group or class setting, self-disclosures are not meant to recount experiences just for the sake of discussion. Instead, they are meant to make a specific point relevant to the subject or to tie together discussion points. There are a couple of different ways to incorporate experiences into content.

- **Ask participants specific questions about their experiences related to the topic.** For example, *"Living with family members, roommates, or housemates often requires the need to negotiate household tasks, what has been your experience with negotiating?"*

    Write down a question or two that you might ask your group members about their relevant experiences for your next group or class.

    _____
    _____
    _____
    _____
    _____
    _____

- **As a peer leader, consider sharing your personal account or experiences as part of your lecture points.** Make sure that your experience relates specifically to your content and exemplifies a point you are trying to make. For example, *"A major move to a new location involves changes in your living situation, your social circle, and your work or school environments. This can be a lot to adjust to all at once. I remember when I moved from Washington to Boston, it took me at least six months to feel settled in my new apt, my new job, and to meet some new friends."*

Identify an example of a personal experience you might share that relates to the content of your next group or class.

_____

_____

_____

_____

_____

- **Recount experiences that participants have shared in prior groups or classes that relate to your group's content or that exemplify specific lecture points.** Be sure that whatever experiences you discuss were public knowledge and initially shared by the group member. For example, *"Last week Stephanie talked about her experience teaching a class for the first time and how she discovered that she did not feel as prepared as she would have liked. Today, we're going to talk about how to organize your activity materials so that you may feel more prepared ahead of time."*

  Identify an example of an experience a participant shared in your group or class that relates to the content of your next group or class.

  _____

  _____

  _____

  _____

  _____

- **Connect a participant's experience to the discussion topic, if not readily obvious.** Respond to the person about the comments, and then make points that tie it back to the class content. If the connection is not apparent to you, you might say, *"That's an interesting experience you have shared. Tell me about how your experience relates to our point about…"* It is crucial to keep the discussions focused on your content.

4.4 Collaborating with Peers

Collaborating with Peers means working together with peers on a project or a group activity. Collaborating signifies that you are working as a team. Collaborating underscores the point that you are working cooperatively in a partnership. In any partnership, each person contributes individual skills and experiences towards a commonly agreed upon goal. Collaborating with peers often joins people together with unique perspectives and experiences in order to achieve a common goal.

© 2009, Trustees of Boston University. All rights reserved. Center for Psychiatric Rehabilitation.

What are the benefits of peer-led groups?

Identify a time when you collaborated with a peer partner. What were the good aspects of your collaboration with a peer leader?

What aspects would you like to have changed in your collaboration with a peer leader?

What learning did you walk away with for future collaborations with peers?

Collaborating with peers involves a few skills:

- **Identify a peer partner to collaborate with in a group activity or class.** Choose someone who:
  - may want to collaborate with you
  - may want to co-lead a group or class
  - may have some natural leadership qualities
  - may have a particular interest or expertise in the topic of your group or class

- **Identify a peer partner or two to collaborate with in your next group activity or class.**

  _____

  _____

- **Plan a strategy for how you will be working together before the group or class starts.** Decide ahead of time:
  - who will take the primary leadership role for particular content areas and activities
  - how you will switch roles of primary leadership
  - how you will present yourselves to the group

  Identify some points regarding your role and your co-leader's role that you might suggest when you plan your working relationship together.

Your Role	*Co-Leader's Role*
_____	_____
_____	_____
_____	_____
_____	_____
_____	_____

- **Work cooperatively with your co-leader during your group or class.** Respect your co-leader's style of teaching and information shared while in the group together. Do not interrupt your co-leader or undermine what he or she is saying in front of the class. Save any points of disagreement for what your co-leader may have said or done until *after* the group or class.

- **Evaluate your collaboration with each other *after* the class or group activity.** Discuss the strengths of your partnership and any aspects that need improvement. Brainstorm ways to improve your working relationship for the next class or group.

© 2009, Trustees of Boston University. All rights reserved. Center for Psychiatric Rehabilitation.

4.5 Supporting Peer Leaders

Supporting Peer Leaders is offering assistance, encouragement, praise, and/or advice to peer leaders. Supporting peer leaders can help to solidify a peer partnership. As our leader, Bill Anthony, has said many times in the past, *"Support, like beauty, is in the eye of the beholder."* Therefore, it is important to identify if and when support is desired and needed. Some techniques for supporting peer leaders entails:

- **Identify the need for support by assessing the peer leader's performance in a group activity.** You may have formal evaluations for group leaders, or your process may be very informal.

    How do you evaluate leaders' performances at your program or agency now?

    _____

    _____

    _____

    _____

    _____

    How might you evaluate leaders' performances differently in the future?

    _____

    _____

    _____

    _____

    _____

    Think of a situation when you have worked with a peer leader. Identify your peer leader's need for support.

    _____

    _____

    _____

    _____

    _____

© 2009, Trustees of Boston University. All rights reserved. Center for Psychiatric Rehabilitation.

- **Identify the desire for support by deciding whether the peer leader would want to receive support from you.** This may depend on your roles and working relationship together. If you suspect that the person may not want to receive support from you, then you may need to address these issues in your relationship of working together.

  Identify your peer leader's desire for support.

  _____
  _____
  _____
  _____
  _____

- **Identify the category of support needed and desired.** Some categories and examples of support are:
  - People, a group leader who serves as a mentor
  - Places, an office to review curriculum before a group or class
  - Things, a computer to prepare class materials
  - Activities, meetings with supervisor and/or group leader to review curriculum

  Identify your peer leader's category of support needs or desires.

  People:
  _____
  _____

  Places:
  _____
  _____

  Things:
  _____
  _____

  Activities:
  _____
  _____

- **Identify the type of support needed and desired.** Some types of support may be:
    — Assistance or help in getting a task accomplished
    — Encouragement or emotional support to proceed in the leadership role
    — Praise for a job well done
    — Advice for how to perform the task differently

    Identify your peer leader's type of support needed and desired.

    Assistance:
    _____
    _____

    Encouragement:
    _____
    _____

    Praise:
    _____
    _____

    Advice:
    _____
    _____

- **Express the support to the peer leader by stating or giving the appropriate type of support.** If you suspect that the support is not fully desired from you, then you may need to practice what to say and how you might express your support to this person.

    Write out what you might say or do to express support to your peer leader.

    _____
    _____
    _____
    _____

This concludes the activity of Promoting Peer Leadership. The checklist for these skills is included on the next page.

© 2009, Trustees of Boston University. All rights reserved. Center for Psychiatric Rehabilitation.

CHECKLIST: Promoting Peer Leadership

Name of Group Leader: _____

Name of Group Activity: _____ Date _____

Encouraged Peer-to-Peer Interactions   ☐ Yes   ☐ No   ☐ Partial

Comments _____
_____
_____

Self-Disclosed   ☐ Yes   ☐ No   ☐ Partial

Comments _____
_____
_____

Incorporated Experiences into Content   ☐ Yes   ☐ No   ☐ Partial

Comments _____
_____
_____

Collaborated with Peers   ☐ Yes   ☐ No   ☐ Partial

Comments _____
_____
_____

Supported Peer Leaders   ☐ Yes   ☐ No   ☐ Partial

Comments _____
_____
_____

CHECKLIST: Promoting Peer Leadership

© 2009, Trustees of Boston University. All rights reserved. Center for Psychiatric Rehabilitation.

Chapter 5: Following Up the Group Activity

5.1	Evaluating the Group Activity
5.2	Assessing Experiences with Participants
5.3	Identifying Future Activities
5.4	Recording Progress Notes or Other Documentation about Group Members' Participation
Checklist:	Following Up the Group Activity

Chapter 5: Following Up the Group Activity

Following up the group activity is done *after* the group activity. Following up the group activity allows you to have closure with the group or class and to consider the future of the group or class. Following up the group activity involves a series of skills:

5.1 Evaluating the Group Activity

5.2 Assessing Experiences with Participants

5.3 Identifying Future Activities

5.4 Recording Progress Notes or Other Documentation about Group Members' Participation

Each one of the follow-up skills will be discussed with explanations and suggestions, and examples and practices will be sprinkled throughout this chapter.

5.1 Evaluating the Group Activity

Evaluating the Group Activity means assessing the effectiveness of your activities in promoting the individuals' participation and progress. Evaluating the group activity provides a way of modifying the activity content to better meet your participants' needs. Evaluating the group activity involves assessing the participants' acquisition of the new knowledge and skills in a couple of ways.

- **Examine the group objectives that were identified originally and reviewed when the class began.** Analyze what the students learned or gained from participating in the group or class. Examining the group objectives helps the leader to decide if the purpose and guidelines for the group's content were met. Objectives may be reviewed by yourself, with your co-leader, and with the group on the last day of your class or session.

    List the objectives that you wrote for your group or class and review them.

    _____

    _____

    _____

    _____

    _____

- **Administer a pre-test and a post-test to the group participants.** It is important to test the students' knowledge of a skill or topic *before* it is taught and to re-test their knowledge *after* it is taught. Questions for the pre-test and post-test should be identical so that comparisons of any changes can be made easily. Only a few questions should be written on the tests in order to gain the basic information about participant's knowledge of the skill or topic.

Example questions for a pre-test and post-test for a class on teaching the skill of *Responding to Feedback* might be:

— What does the skill Responding to Feedback mean to you?

— What is the benefit of Responding to Feedback?

— What are the steps for how to Respond to Feedback?

— When would you need to Respond to Feedback?

Example questions for a pre-test and post-test for a knowledge-based class on an introduction to psychiatric rehabilitation might be:

— What is the mission statement of psychiatric rehabilitation?

— What are three of the values of psychiatric rehabilitation?

— What is the basic principle of psychiatric rehabilitation?

Identify some questions for a pre-test and post-test for your class or group.

_____

_____

_____

_____

_____

_____

5.2 Assessing Experiences with Participants

Assessing Experiences with Participants is reviewing the students' thoughts and feelings about the group or class. As the group leader, you will notice people's reactions during each session. You also will need to ask for feedback about their experiences at the end of the group session or class. There are a couple of ways to assess experiences with participants.

- **Observe the group members participation and performance throughout the class or group sessions.** Notes regarding these observations should be taken mentally or written down throughout the teaching process. Some adjustments to content and/or teaching style can be made in the moment, while others may need to be made in the future.

- **Request feedback from the participants during the last day of the class or group session.** This may be done informally through a group discussion, and/or you may create a written feedback form. Some sample questions might include:

    — What did you like best about this class or group?

    — What did you dislike?

    — What suggestions do you have to improve this class or group?

Identify some feedback questions for your class or group.

___

5.3 Identifying Future Activities

Identifying Future Activities is planning how and what to teach in the class or group in the future. Identifying the future activities is deciding what worked well in the group in order to be repeated the next time and what changes need to be made to improve the group or class the next time.

- **Review the activity content that was taught in the group or class by compiling the information from the pre-tests and post-tests.** Based on the results, decide on what activities could be continued, deleted, and/or improved for a future class or group. Activity content areas might include the:

    — Amount of information covered or taught

    — Specific teaching points of the content

    — Demonstrations and examples shown

    — Practice exercises

    Identify some changes or future activities from your last group or class.

___

© 2009, Trustees of Boston University. All rights reserved. Center for Psychiatric Rehabilitation.

- **Review the feedback from the participants about their experiences.** Based on the results, decide on how the group process could stay the same or could be modified, changed, or improved for a future class or group. Group process aspects might include the:
    - Group format
    - Group structure
    - Behavioral expectations
    - Class objectives
    - Teaching pace
    - Group leaders

    Identify some changes in the group process from your last group or class.

    _____
    _____
    _____
    _____
    _____

5.4 Recording Progress Notes or Other Documentation about Group Members' Participation

Recording progress notes or other documentation allows you to have evidence of each individual's progress and participation in a group or class.

Often agencies and programs require regular and specific progress notes about group members' participation in activities. Progress notes may need to be written after each class or group session as well as at the end of a series of classes. Any additional documentation, like pre-tests, post-tests, and feedback forms may need to be kept in each group member's file.

Agencies also may need to have documentation written about each group or class. Learning objectives often are required as well as evaluation forms. Supervision notes and performance evaluations also may be required for each group leader.

What procedures for documentation are required at your agency?

_____
_____
_____
_____
_____

© 2009, Trustees of Boston University. All rights reserved. Center for Psychiatric Rehabilitation.

How might you want to change the procedures for the future?

_____
_____
_____
_____
_____
_____
_____
_____
_____
_____
_____
_____
_____
_____

This concludes the final section on Following-Up the Group Activity. The corresponding checklist for your use and for your supervisor's use is included on the next page.

CHECKLIST: Following Up the Group Activity

Name of Group Leader: _____

Name of Group Activity: _____ Date _____

Evaluated the Group Activity   ☐ Yes   ☐ No   ☐ Partial

Comments _____

_____

_____

_____

Assessed Experiences with Participants   ☐ Yes   ☐ No   ☐ Partial

Comments _____

_____

_____

_____

Identified Future Activities   ☐ Yes   ☐ No   ☐ Partial

Comments _____

_____

_____

_____

Recorded Progress Notes or Other Documentation about Group Members' Participation

     ☐ Yes   ☐ No   ☐ Partial

Comments _____

_____

_____

_____

Conclusion

Group Process Guidelines for Leading Groups and Classes was designed to provide you with some guidelines, information, and skills for leading groups and classes. After reading the guidelines and examples as well as completing the exercises and checklists in this workbook, you will have learned the basic skills of facilitating a group or class. These guidelines included the preparation skills, delivery skills, and follow-up skills involved in leading a knowledge-based or skills-based group or class.

The chapter on promoting peer leaders was designed to encourage more peer-to-peer interactions within a group or class, to collaborate with peer leaders, and to support peer leaders. Peer leaders provide a special role and offer valuable contributions in leading and co-leading groups and classes. We appreciate the strength peer leaders have shown through their lived experiences that they share in groups as well as their inspiration as role models to others.

Learning to feel comfortable and confident with group process takes time and experience. To become skillful at leading a group or class, you will need to practice with the support of someone more experienced than you, as a group leader. Having support as you learn to facilitate a group or class is very important. The support that a mentor can provide can enhance your achieving confidence and competency in teaching classes and leading groups. If you have received training in group process, the person who did the training might be willing to mentor you. Also, there may be other group leaders who currently are teaching classes in your agency or community. There is so much we can learn from other group leaders. Each leader has his or her own style, strengths, and techniques in facilitating groups and classes.

The components of a good learning model include acquiring information, skills, practice, and supervision. The checklists at the end of each chapter can be extremely useful in structuring an objective self-assessment of the group process skills or an evaluation by a supervisor. The practice and supervision are important because they will help you to grow in competency and to gain confidence in your ability to become a valued group leader.

Best wishes as you lead groups and classes effectively and successfully in the future.

© 2009, Trustees of Boston University. All rights reserved. Center for Psychiatric Rehabilitation.

References

Anderson, S. C., & Mandell, D. L. (1989). The use of self-disclosure by professional social workers. *Social Casework: The Journal of Contemporary Social Work,* 259–267.

Andrews, H. B. (1995). *Group design and leadership.* Boston: Allyn & Bacon.

Anthony, W. A., & Huckshorn, K. A. (2008). *Principled leadership in mental health systems and programs.* Boston: Boston University, Center for Psychiatric Rehabilitation.

Carkhuff, R.R. (1981). *The LEAST approach to classroom discipline.* The Michigan Project and Northern Michigan University.

Carkhuff, R.R. (2000). *The art of helping, 8th edition.* Amherst, MA: HRD Press.

Cohen, M., Danley, D., & Nemec, P. (1985, 2007). *Psychiatric rehabilitation training technology: Direct skills teaching.* Boston: Boston University, Center for Psychiatric Rehabilitation.

Cohen, M., Farkas, M., & Cohen, B. (1986, 2007). *Psychiatric rehabilitation training technology: Functional assessment.* Boston: Boston University, Center for Psychiatric Rehabilitation.

Cohen, M., Farkas, M., Cohen, B., & Unger, K. (1991, 2007). *Psychiatric rehabilitation training technology: Setting an overall rehabilitation goal.* Boston: Boston University, Center for Psychiatric Rehabilitation.

Cohen, M., Nemec, P., & Farkas, M. (2000). *Psychiatric rehabilitation training technology: Connecting for rehabilitation readiness.* Boston: Boston University, Center for Psychiatric Rehabilitation.

Cohen, M., Nemec, P., Farkas, M., Forbess, R., & Cohen, B. (1988, 2007). *Training technology: Case management.* Boston: Boston University, Center for Psychiatric Rehabilitation.

Copeland, M. E. (2000). *Wellness recovery action plan.* Peach Press.

Corey, M. S., & Corey, G. (1997, 5th edition). *Groups, process, and practice.* New York: Brookes-Cole.

Forbess, R. (2006). *Rehabilitation group activity: Preparation and delivery guide.* Boston: Boston University, Center for Psychiatric Rehabilitation.

Gagne, C., & Gayler, C. (2007). *Louisiana personal assistance services training of trainers.* Boston: Boston University, Center for Psychiatric Rehabilitation.

Rutan, J. S., & Stone, W. N. (1993, 2nd edition). *Psychodynamic group psychotherapy.* New York: Guilford Press.

Spaniol, L. (2008). What would a recovery-oriented program look like? *International Journal of Psychosocial Rehabilitation. 13*(1), 57–66.

Spaniol, L., Koehler, M., & Hutchinson, D. (1994, 2009). *The recovery workbook: Practical coping and empowerment strategies for people with psychiatric disabilities.* Boston: Boston University, Center for Psychiatric Rehabilitation.

Spaniol, L., Koehler, M., & Hutchinson, D. (1994). *Leader's guide—The recovery workbook: Practical coping and empowerment strategies for people with psychiatric disability.* Boston: Boston University, Center for Psychiatric Rehabilitation.